W9-ANQ-219

Modern Operational
Circuit Design

MODERN OPERATIONAL CIRCUIT DESIGN

John I. Smith

WILEY-INTERSCIENCE

a division of John Wiley & Sons, Inc.
New York • London • Sydney • Toronto

To Master David Dylan Smith

Preface

This book addresses the practicing technologist who is not conversant with electronics. It presents a body of techniques that has application in every field of science and industry, including the social sciences and even the arts.

The argument is set forth in English and in Graphics. Some electrical knowledge is presupposed, but it is thought to be of the axiomatic kind that is difficult to avoid in an electrified culture. Indeed, half-serious thought was given to the subtitle: "Ohm's Law with Applications."

Reading this book should by all means be accompanied by direct experience with the attractive hardware it advocates; a glance ahead to Chapter 15 is thus in order.

Here is the hardware end of a part of Norbert Wiener's science. The book seeks to be practical by providing the most practical of all commodities—insight.

John I. Smith

Washington, D.C.
April 1971

Acknowledgments

Many of the advanced circuits in this book had their genesis when I was associated with Professor Gene Simmons in the M.I.T. Department of Earth and Planetary Sciences.

The advice and encouragement of Mr. Michael Chessman were vital in the formative stages.

I came of age professionally at the time of the introduction of the 2N 930 transistor. I thank the three men who shaped me: George Biernson, Paul Johannesson, and Roy Sallen—all of the Sylvania Applied Research Laboratory. Thanks are due to R. A. Pease, P. D. Hansen, Bruce Seddon, and D. H. Sheingold of George A. Philbrick Researches. A note of special gratitude to James C. Hosken of GAP/R.

Of lesser degree but vital was my association with Hans Hug, Thor Knutred, and Meyer Press of the Sylvania laboratory and with Harvey Fox of Keltron Corporation.

J. I. S.

Contents

Modern Operational
Circuit Design

Chapter I

The Unity-Gain Invertor

In operational circuitry voltages of positive and negative polarities represent positive and negative values of signals, respectively. A signal may be the measured value of a physical quantity obtaining from moment to moment or it may represent the value of a variable in a system being modeled or simulated; in the most abstract case the positive or negative (or zero) value of the signal voltage denotes an algebraic number in an equation or set of equations being solved.

The output terminal of an operational amplifier must be able to range both positive and negative with respect to zero volts (ground potential). Accordingly, both plus and minus power supply voltages are provided to the amplifier. Operational amplifiers are dc amplifiers; this means that unchanging or very slowly changing signals are treated in the same way as rapidly varying signals. For example, the very slowly changing terminal voltage of a battery being charged may be amplified with the same ease as the voltage fluctuation representing a sound wave. In fact, unchanging sources such as batteries are used in the early examples, for simplicity and to emphasize that direct voltages are entirely valid as input signals. Another way to state this circuit property is to say that there is no inherent low-frequency limit to the circuit response—dc or "zero-frequency" signals are welcome.

It is necessary to distinguish the operational amplifier from the operational circuit in which it is embedded and of which it is a part. An apparent paradox is that the circuit performance is largely independent of the amplifier properties and that to make it more so is the chief goal of the amplifier designer. The distinction is set forth in Figure

1

1.1, which shows an operational amplifier used in one of the more common operational circuits. The operational circuit has an input terminal coming from a signal source, e_s, and an output terminal that impresses an output voltage, e_o, on a load impedance, Z_L. The load impedance does not appear in the operational equation for the excellent reason that the circuit is independent of load, within wide limits, this being a salient virtue of feedback technology. The operational amplifier has two input terminals and one output terminal. An algebraic sign attaches to each input and requires interpretation: the minus sign identifies the *inverting* input; voltages at this input appear at the output not only

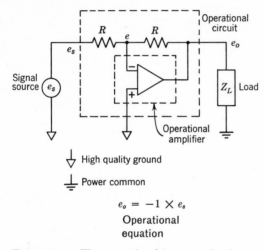

$$e_o = -1 \times e_s$$
Operational
equation

Figure 1.1.   The operational invertor circuit.

amplified but also with a reversal of sign. The plus sign denotes the *noninverting* or *direct* input; voltages here are amplified without change of sign. For the moment, only the inverting input is employed, the direct input being connected to high-quality ground. The output of the operational amplifier here coincides with the output of the operational circuit, as is frequently but not invariably the case.

In studying this operational circuit the objective is an early, thorough comprehension of its functioning. The plan of attack has three parts: (1) a statement of what the circuit does, (2) a brief description of how it functions, and (3) an exhaustive explanation of why it so behaves.

In Figure 1.1 an operational amplifier is connected to invert or take the negative of the input signal. The output voltage, e_o, is precisely the signal or source voltage, e_s, with its polarity changed. If the signal is negative the output will be positive but equal in magnitude. This relationship obtains at all instants of time. A time history of a typical signal is shown in Figure 1.2 together with the corresponding output voltage. The output voltage is the mirror image of the input signal.

A facile preliminary understanding of the invertor circuit may be achieved by accepting two assertions: (1) the amplifier input terminal allows no current to flow into or out of it and (2) the action of the feedback is such that the voltage at the inverting input, e, is zero. These assumptions are to be justified and qualified in the sequel.

If one end of a resistor is at zero volts, a current flows in the resistor which is proportional to the voltage at the other end. The input resistor

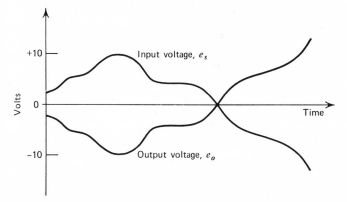

Figure 1.2. Input and output of circuit of Figure 1.1.

in Figure 1.1 is just so arranged; its right-hand terminal is at zero volts by reason of assertion 2, and thus a current proportional to the source voltage flows in it. The input resistor connected in this way can be thought of as a voltage-to-current transducer.

Since assertion 1 prohibits the current from flowing into the amplifier, where does this current flow? The only path is the feedback resistor, of which the left-hand terminal is connected to a known voltage, namely zero, by assertion 2. The right-hand terminal is connected to the amplifier output voltage, e_o. What must the output voltage be in order to draw off the current arriving by way of the input resistor? It must be *equal* in magnitude to the source voltage and *opposite* in polarity.

The argument above assumes that the input and feedback resistors have identical ohmic values, R. A hint of what is to come is provided by letting the feedback resistor have the value $2R$. It should be clear that the output must then swing twice as far in voltage in order to

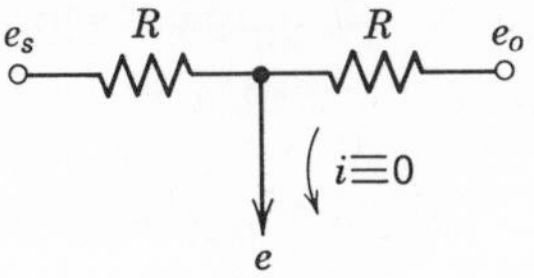

$$e = \frac{e_s + e_o}{2}$$

if $i \equiv 0$

Figure 1.3.   Voltage averaging network.

carry off the current; the result of making the feedback resistor $10R$ or $100R$ should be equally plain. In short, here is an amplifying circuit the magnification factor of which is set by the ratio of two resistors.

Apart from the amplifier the operational circuit of Figure 1.1 comprises only the two-resistor network isolated in Figure 1.3. The input signal is applied to one resistor and the amplifier output voltage to the other; the midpoint of the network is connected to the inverting input of the amplifier. Because the amplifier input draws no current and because the resistors are equal in value, the voltage at their midpoint, e, is simply the average of the two impressed voltages. The operational circuit operates in such a way as to make the voltage e go to zero; that is, a point of stable equilibrium exists at $e = 0$. Observe that this will be so only if $e_o = -e_s$; the average of two voltages is zero only if they are equal and opposite in sign.

Thus an equilibrium exists for that value of the output voltage that renders the amplifier input voltage zero. To justify this assertion the inner workings of the operational amplifier must be defined. Figure 1.4 exhibits a block diagram of this internal functioning. The operational amplifier is taken to consist in a time integrator, a voltage gain ω_H, and a sign inversion.* It suffices for the moment to observe that (1)

---

* A note of encouragement is offered to certain readers: integral calculus is one of the mathematical disciplines that operational circuitry exploits and, in the process, rather demolishes as a barrier to understanding.

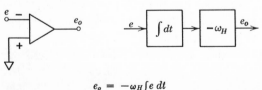

$$e_o = -\omega_H \int e\, dt$$

Figure 1.4.   Block diagram characterization for the operational amplifier.

the output of an integrator is constant when its input is zero (the integral of zero is a constant), and (2) when the input is V volts, then the output rate of change is V volts per second (the time integral of a constant is a ramp function). These properties, together with the sign reversal, suffice to demonstrate the stable equilibrium.

If the output voltage is at the equilibrium value, then $e = 0$ and the integrator output is unchanging. If the output is not sufficiently negative, then $e > 0$, and, because of the sign reversal, the integrator causes the output voltage to change in the negative direction. The reverse is true when the output voltage is more negative than the equilibrium value. Thus an off-equilibrium condition produces action that drives toward the equilibrium state.

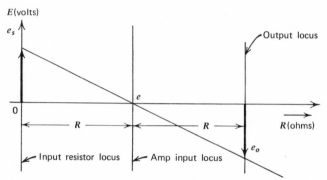

Figure 1.5.   Voltage-resistance plot for the circuit of Figure 1.1.

The preceding ideas are vivid in graphical form. Figure 1.5 is a plot of voltage versus resistance for the invertor circuit at equilibrium. This is *not* the usual voltage-current plot; the ordinate is voltage and the abscissa is resistance. Current, the ratio of the two, appears as the *slope* of the inclined line in the diagram. The source voltage is plotted on the vertical axis. The inverting input of the amplifier appears at a distance R ohms to the right of the origin, R being the value of the input resistor. The voltage of the inverting input is plotted as zero by assertion 2. The output voltage locus is a vertical line appearing at a farther distance, R ohms, to the right, the distance representing the value of the feedback resistor. The sloping line represents both the current flowing in the input resistor and that which must flow in the feedback resistor, because no current enters or leaves by way of the input terminal. This line intersects the output locus to determine the output voltage. Nothing more obscure than the laws of Ohm and Kirchoff is involved, as is suggested by the simple form of the diagram. The same technique of graphical analysis is used in Figures 1.6 and 1.7 to reveal gain factors other than unity. From these diagrams it is clear why invertor circuits have been called "electronic levers" by a distinguished pioneer in the field.

The amplifier characterization of Figure 1.4 is well suited to the description of the dynamic response of operational circuits. In particular, the step response is instructive. The intent is not to discuss dynamics

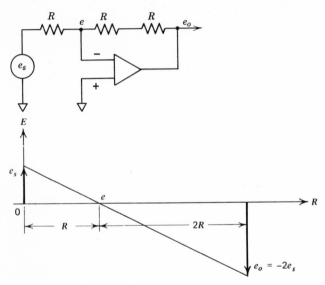

Figure 1.6.   Gain of −2.

for its own sake, but rather to make plain the *sequential* nature of events in the feedback loop. A chronic obstacle to the understanding of feedback has been the supposed simultaneity of events within the loop. Indeed, if the output is known to depend in part on itself, it is easy to imagine the confusion caused by the impression that "everything happens at once." In actuality, physical systems do not respond instantly and the vexing simultaneity is but an illusion.

Figure 1.1 has been redrawn in Figure 1.8. The signal source, e_s, has been particularized into a 1-volt battery and a single-pole double-throw switch. The switch is presumed to be thrown at time zero to

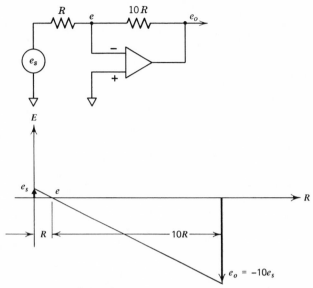

Figure 1.7.   Gain of −10.

give the voltage-versus-time history depicted in Figure 1.9a. Initially the circuit is in equilibrium with all three voltages equal to zero. At time zero the signal jumps to +1 volt. The output voltage is unchanged. Consequently the input voltage, e, which is the average of the other two, jumps to +0.5 volt. The output changes in the negative direction in a manner governed by the block diagram of Figure 1.4. The output of the time integrator is initially a ramp of −0.5 volt/second. The coefficient block labeled ω_H in Figure 1.4 represents a numerical constant multiplier having a typical value of 10^7 for an ordinary operational

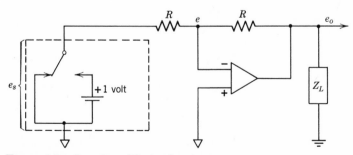

Figure 1.8.   Invertor with step input source.

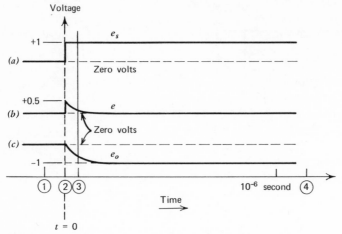

Figure 1.9a. Voltage-time histories in circuit of Figure 1.8.

amplifier. The combined effect of the two functional blocks is that the output e_o moves negatively at an initial rate of five million volts per second—a somewhat unsettling number usually written 5 V/μsec (volts per microsecond). This is the initial value only and is immediately and progressively reduced by feedback through the voltage averaging network; that is, the fact of output response reduces the "error signal,"

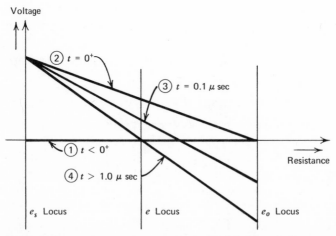

Figure 1.9b. Voltage-resistance plot for four instants during step response of circuit of Figure 1.8.

e, and thus moderates the rate of response. Curves *b* and *c* of Figure 1.9*a* approach 0 and −1, respectively, in asymptotic fashion.

These response curves are the classical decaying exponential functions associated with systems described by first-order linear differential equations. The amplifier, having a single integration, behaves as do physical systems having one energy storage element. Other properties of these curves merit attention. The ordinate of curve *b* records the negative of the slope of curve *c* at every instant. Conversely, curve *c* measures the negative of the area under curve *b*, as a proper integrator should. Furthermore, after 1 or 2 microseconds the input voltage *e* has returned to zero. Assertion 2 is thus justified, although subject still to qualifications of a subtle sort to be developed in later chapters.

It is customary to refer to the inverting input as a "virtual ground." It is called a ground because it remains at (very nearly) zero volts potential. It is "virtual" in that a passive, low-resistance path to actual ground does not exist; the behavior of this point emulates a ground because of the action of the feedback loop. Note that if the amplifier input is regarded as representing a resistance to ground, which is an adequate first approximation for all amplifier types, then assertion 2 implies assertion 1; that is, zero voltage causes zero current in even a low resistance. The two assertions are seen to be consonant with each other, even if neither has been proved with rigor.

Various instants during the response to the step input can be plotted on a voltage-resistance graph to give a graphical résumé of events during the transient (see Figure 1.9*b*).

The time-integrator property attributed to the operational amplifier must be contradistinguished from the closed-loop operational circuit of the same name, to be introduced in Chapter 3. They are similar processes, but the one operates within the other, as is set forth at some length in Chapter 10. Furthermore, certain valuable types of operational amplifier depart from the simple integrator characteristic given here, which modifies the explanation; but these matters are best deferred, or better still, the onus transferred to the maker of the apparatus in question.

Chapter II

Inverting Amplifier Circuitry

Figures 1.6 and 1.7 show graphical solutions for inverting amplifier circuits having gains of 2 and 10. It is understood that the solutions depict the situation at a particular instant, namely, when the input source has some positive value. Figure 2.1 shows several instants between which the signal varies, for example, sinusoidally. Note solution 3 for which the input is zero. Furthermore, note that the gain n is any positive real number. Why use fractional gain? Of what use is an "amplifier" with a gain less than 1? It was remarked earlier that the performance of an operational circuit was independent of load—here is a case in point. Concretely, Figure 2.2 shows a precision attenuator; it is a voltage divider that is immune to loading errors and that inverts as well as divides. The load current is supplied by the operational amplifier, which will drive any load within its rating without affecting the accuracy of the operation performed.

The voltage null at the inverting input has several strikingly useful consequences. A resistor connected to the inverting input meters a current to it that depends only on the voltage applied to the other end of the resistor. That is, by Ohm's law, the current that flows in a grounded resistor is proportional to the applied voltage. The resistor serves as a voltage-to-current transducer. Several resistors so connected *do not affect each other;* they are said to be decoupled. The several currents add by simply flowing together and the result is a current delivered

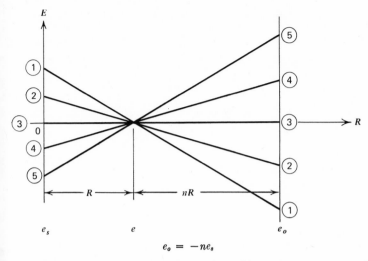

$$e_o = -ne_s$$

Figure 2.1. Gain of $-n$ for various values of instantaneous source voltage.

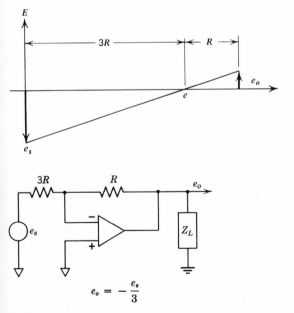

$$e_o = -\frac{e_s}{3}$$

Figure 2.2. Precise 3:1 attenuator and invertor.

to the inverting input which is proportional to the sum of the several source voltages. See Figure 2.3. The sum in question is the algebraic sum, because if a signal voltage is negative it causes a current flow against the arrow, hence makes a negative contribution to the sum. As stated previously, currents delivered to the inverting input can leave by only one path: the feedback resistor. The feedback resistor resembles the input resistors in that one end is connected to virtual ground. Accord-

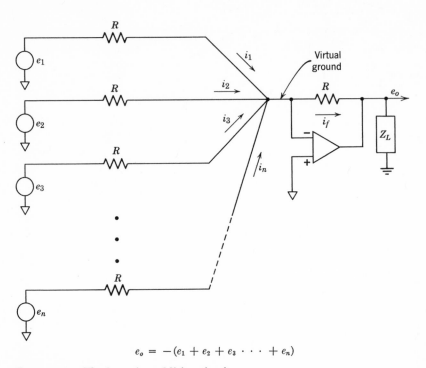

$$e_o = -(e_1 + e_2 + e_3 \cdots + e_n)$$

Figure 2.3.   The inverting addition circuit.

ingly, Ohm's law requires that the other end, the end connected to the output, shall be at a voltage such as to draw off the delivered current.

Thus three continuous processes may be identified as parts of the computation of an algebraic sum:

1. Voltage-to-current conversion in each of the input resistors.
2. Current summation by confluence at the inverting input (which is also called the *summing point* for precisely this reason).
3. Current-to-voltage conversion in the feedback resistor.

Signal inversion is inherent and is convenient in practice as often as it is not.

The behavior of the operational circuit is described above without explicit reference to the amplifier. By its creation of the virtual ground, and by its driving of the load, which is the useful output, the amplifier brings about a situation in which it itself can almost be ignored.

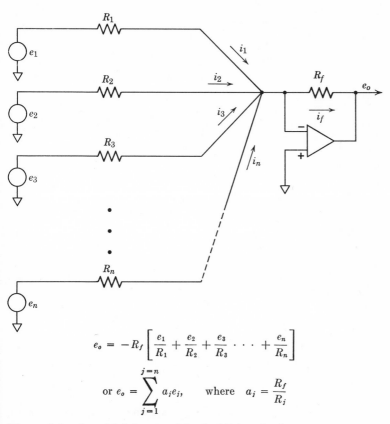

$$e_o = -R_f \left[\frac{e_1}{R_1} + \frac{e_2}{R_2} + \frac{e_3}{R_3} \cdots + \frac{e_n}{R_n} \right]$$

$$\text{or } e_o = \sum_{j=1}^{j=n} a_j e_j, \quad \text{where} \quad a_j = \frac{R_f}{R_j}$$

Figure 2.4. A multiple-input weighted addition circuit.

In Figure 2.3 all the resistors are shown to be equal. If the feedback resistor is made n times larger than the input resistors, an adding circuit having an amplification factor n is the result. This is so because the output voltage must swing n times further in voltage to draw a given current through the feedback resistor. This fact underlies the facile rule that the gain of an operational adder is the ratio of the feedback resistor to the input resistors.

The most general summation circuit is given in Figure 2.4. The several inputs are weighted according to the reciprocal of their resistor values. The operating principles are exactly as before; indeed, the circuit reduces to the simple adder by choosing all resistances equal, and further to the invertor by setting all sources except one equal to zero. No practicality is lost by generality. The number of inputs is without limit; so is the input voltage, provided that suitable input resistors are used. The output is limited as to both voltage and current, but these limits are not confining to the informed user. This circuit has been called the

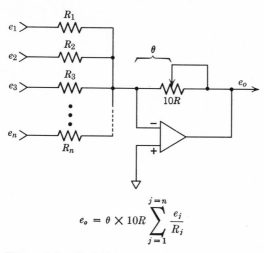

$$e_o = \theta \times 10R \sum_{j=1}^{j=n} \frac{e_j}{R_j}$$

Figure 2.5.   Variable-gain weighted addition circuit.

Linear Combinor; perhaps Polynomial Operator would serve. Suitable names for circuits are important, for an apt name often reveals applications that might not be recognized.

Finally, adjustable gain may be added by making the feedback resistor variable, as in Figure 2.5; furthermore the gain is linear with resistance and hence with fractional rotation, θ, of a potentiometer connected as shown. Calibration is convenient; a multiturn precision potentiometer with a turns-counting dial is appropriate. The gain is adjustable from 0 to 10 with the values shown.

Frequently a continuous reading of a resistance or conductance (reciprocal resistance) is needed. Conversion of resistance and conductance to voltage is provided by the circuits shown in Figures 2.6 and 2.7.

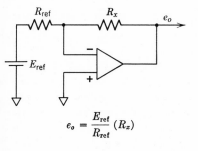

$$e_o = \frac{E_{ref}}{R_{ref}}(R_x)$$

$$e_o = E_{ref}R_{ref}(G_x)$$

$$\text{where } G_x = \frac{1}{R_x}$$

Figure 2.6. Resistance readout circuit.

Figure 2.7. Conductance readout circuit.

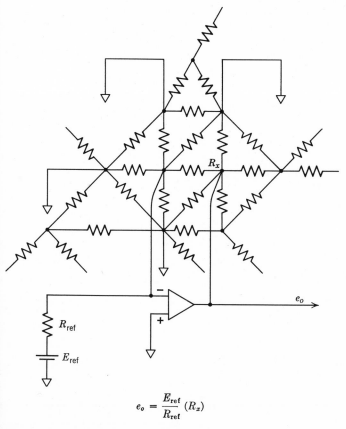

$$e_o = \frac{E_{ref}}{R_{ref}}(R_x)$$

Figure 2.8. In-circuit resistance readout.

15

A reference voltage source and reference resistor of the required accuracy are needed.

The circuit illustrated in Figure 2.6 leads to an elegant method of measuring a resistor in the circuit, a technique of practical value for printed circuits and perhaps for integrated networks. Figure 2.8 shows an unknown resistor, R_x, being measured while embedded in a network. The summing point of the operational amplifier is connected to one end of the unknown and the output to the other. All nodes of the network that connect to the summing point are grounded. Since the summing point is a virtual ground, only the unknown resistor carries current, because the voltage drop across the others is zero. Thus all test current flows in the unknown resistor and, since it is in the feedback, the output voltage is directly proportional to its resistance. The output simply drives the requisite current into the other network components connected to it.

This is trickery of the very best sort, and should prove to be provocative of thought.

Chapter III

The Integrator and Differentiator

One of the troublesome truisms is that a capacitor cannot conduct a direct current. The equivalent of Ohm's law for capacitance holds that the current through a capacitor is proportional to the rate of change of voltage across it. If a constant rate of change of voltage obtains, a constant current will flow. See Figure 3.1.

It has been stated that the operational amplifier maintains its inverting input, called the summing point, at ground potential and that all currents flowing to this point from signal sources must exit via the feedback path. That is, the amplifier implicitly produces the output voltage that is appropriate to prevent the accumulation of charge at the summing point. This statement holds for whatever input variation and for whatever kind of element is placed in the feedback path. In particular, Figure 3.2 shows the invertor configuration except that a capacitor replaces the resistor in the feedback. The resulting circuit is the heart of the electronic differential analyzer and of much else. A mundane example is the ramp generator of Figure 3.3. The 1-volt source causes a current of 1 microampere to flow in the 1-megohm input resistor. The switch is initially closed, connecting the output to the summing point. The 1 microampere flows from the output through the switch to the summing point, and then into the resistor; the amplifier is said to be tightly fed back; the circuit gain is zero and so is the output voltage. When the switch is opened the capacitor must carry the 1 microampere. By

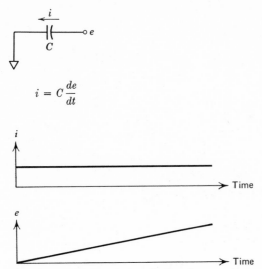

$$i = C\frac{de}{dt}$$

Figure 3.1.   Volt-ampere law for the capacitor.

Figure 3.1 a 1-volt-per-second change in the output voltage suffices to drive the 1 microampere through the 1-microfarad capacitor. The integrator in Figure 3.3 is called a real-time or 1-second integrator because 1 volt in produces 1 volt-per-second out.

The integrator performance equation is derived by setting the current in the input resistor equal to the current in the feedback capacitor (Figure 3.2).

The ramp generator converts elapsed time to voltage, the zero of time and voltage occurring at the instant the switch is opened. If the amplifier

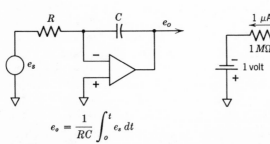

$$e_o = \frac{1}{RC}\int_o^t e_s\,dt$$

Figure   3.2.   The   operational integrator.

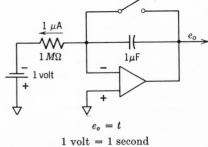

$$e_o = t$$
1 volt = 1 second

Figure 3.3.   The integrator as a ramp generator.

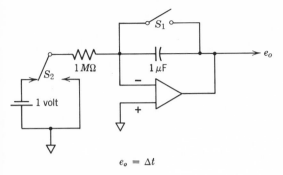

$$e_o = \Delta t$$

Figure 3.4. Intervalometer.

has a 10-volt output range, a ramp of up to 10 seconds can be generated with this circuit. The accuracy of the time-to-voltage conversion is usually limited by the passive elements, not by the amplifier.

The step from a ramp generator to an interval timer is short and will be taken here because it typifies the almost freewheeling innovation invited by this technology. See Figure 3.4. A second switch S_2 connects the input resistor to the reference source only during the interval to be measured, it being connected to ground (zero volts) at all other times. Switch S_1 is closed momentarily prior to the measurement in order to bring the output to zero by discharging the capacitor. The switch S_1 is called a reset switch. After the interval of interest, when S_2 returns to ground, the integrator holds the voltage of the final instant because the integral of zero is a constant. This voltage may be read on a meter, fed to an analog-to-digital converter, or perhaps used as an input to some process—computational, instrumental, or other.

The applications of the time integrator given above are mundane because of the prosaic nature of the inputs. The glory of this circuit is

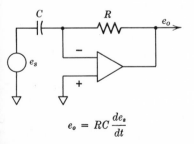

$$e_o = RC \frac{de_s}{dt}$$

Figure 3.5. The operational differentiator.

the accuracy with which *any* signal may be integrated in *real time*. Its ubiquitous utility will become plain.

If a resistor and a capacitor suffice for an integrator, the inverse operation, differentiation, should not be difficult. It is done by interchanging the two components as shown in Figure 3.5. The equation is derived in the same way as for the integrator; it is in fact the same equation with the roles of input and output variables interchanged. In practice, integration is preferred to differentiation when there is a choice. The differentiator is used in situations where the rate of change of an existing signal is to be instrumented.

A review is in order; sufficient operational circuitry has been described to form a modest list:

1. Inversion, or multiplication by −1.
2. Multiplication by any negative real constant.
3. Addition, including weighted addition.
4. Measurement of resistance and conductance, including *in situ* measurement.
5. Integration and differentiation with respect to time.

Collectively these operations enable the solution of linear algebraic and differential equations and the implementation of an impressive fraction of the tasks in instrumentation, simulation, computation, regulation, and control.

Chapter IV

The Follower and
Follower-with-Gain

So far only inverting circuits have been discussed. These circuits have three traits in common:

1. The output voltage is the negative of the input signal or signals.
2. Only the inverting input of the amplifier is used explicitly, the other input being grounded.
3. A virtual ground is made to exist by the action of feedback.

In this chapter the second large class of operational circuitry is introduced:

1. The output voltage has the same sign as the input signal.
2. Both the direct and the inverting inputs are used explicitly.
3. A virtual open circuit is brought about by feedback action.

The generic name is the Voltage Follower or simply follower. Item 3, the open circuit property, best typifies the follower; almost all of the elaborations of the circuit depend on it.

It is well known that voltmeters should not draw current from the source or circuit they measure. In other words, a voltmeter that draws current is said to load the measured circuit. Vacuum tube voltmeters are preferred to ordinary meters for this reason. There are two approaches to the loading problem. The first is to use a very high resistance meter; the second is to prevent current flow by balancing or bucking

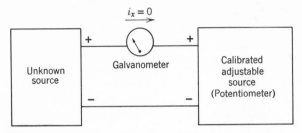

Figure 4.1.   A potentiometric voltage measurement.

out the unknown voltage with an equal and opposite voltage in the measuring instrument. The latter is the classical Potentiometer. In Figure 4.1 an adjustable voltage source is used to buck out the unknown source potential so as to make the current indicated by the galvanometer zero. When the current is nulled to zero the true electric potential of the unknown (also called its open-circuit voltage) is read off the calibrated dials of the Potentiometer. Because no current flows a true open-circuit condition obtains even though a physical closed circuit is connected. Put another way, the ohmic voltage drops or IR drops in the unknown, in the potentiometer, and even in the hookup leads all vanish because the current is zero.

The potentiometric method has been automated electromechanically and electronically. In the first, a servomechanism drives the adjustable source toward voltage equilibrium or the equivalent, a current null; this is the basis of the traditional slide-wire stripchart recorder. The electronic embodiment depends on an amplifier having an input-output relationship, or gain, of positive unity, as indicated in Figure 4.2. Such an amplifier renders a real resistor R of whatever value into a virtual open circuit, because the amplifier insures that the two ends of the resistor are always at the same voltage and thus that the current through the resistor is zero. This virtual open circuit is the exact dual of the virtual ground described in Chapter 1, and is brought about by the

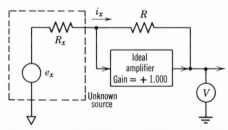

Figure 4.2.   Impedance multiplication by bootstrapping.

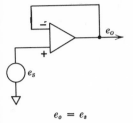

$$e_o = e_s$$

Figure 4.3. The unity-gain voltage follower.

operational amplifier in a completely analogous way. A resistor thus manipulated is said to be *bootstrapped*.

The positive unity-gain amplifier circuit is the *voltage follower;* the name forms a nomenclatural link to the venerable cathode follower. Indeed the operational follower is the ultimate refinement thereof; it shares the attributes of high-input and low-output impedance; additionally it features precise unity gain and freedom from macroscopic voltage offset between input and output. (The word *precise* and its relatives apply to operational circuitry in the same spirit and with the same quantitative significance as in the machine tool industry.)

The follower is seen in Figure 4.3 to be the simplest operational circuit—only a connection from output to inverting input. Schematic elegance aside, this circuit introduces a whole new class of circuitry in which *both* inputs are active. A differential operational amplifier is required; aforementioned circuits may be implemented with a single-ended amplifier—one that possesses only the inverting input. The differential operational amplifier is more general than the single-ended type, to which it reduces when its direct (+) input is grounded.

The block diagram of Figure 1.4 is extended to the differential case in Figure 4.4. The inverting input voltage e is replaced by the differential

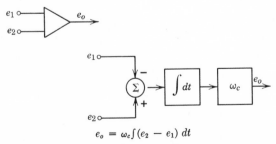

$$e_o = \omega_c \int (e_2 - e_1)\, dt$$

Figure 4.4. Block diagram characterization for the differential operational amplifier.

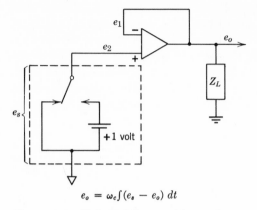

$$e_o = \omega_c \int (e_s - e_o)\, dt$$

Figure 4.5.   Voltage follower with step input source.

input voltage $e_2 - e_1$. A differential amplifier responds to the difference in voltage between its two inputs; it does *not* respond to the gross voltage at the inputs, only to the difference between them. For example, if the direct input voltage is 9.0001 and the inverting input voltage is 9.0000, then the amplifier responds to $(e_2 - e_1)$ which equals 0.0001 volt. As before, the amplifier produces the time integral of the input voltage; a differential voltage produces a rate of change of voltage at the output.

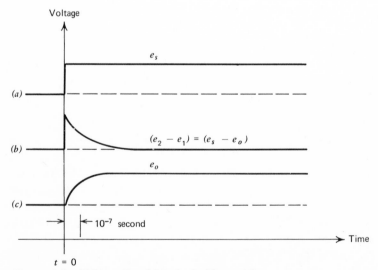

Figure 4.6.   Voltage-time histories in Figure 4.5.

The operation of the voltage follower is fundamentally identical with that of the invertor, and this identity will be emphasized by a parallel presentation. (In fact, complete functional and structural isomorphism occurs in the follower-with-gain circuit to be presented next.) The circuit and the waveforms for a step input are shown in Figures 4.5 and 4.6. The amplifier actuation voltage, curve b, is simply the difference between input and output, and when this difference approaches zero, the output

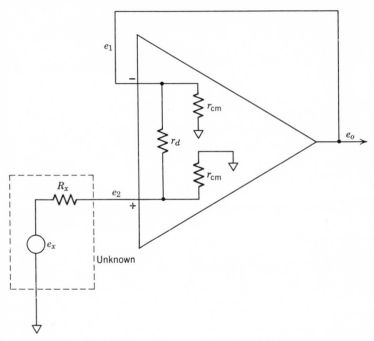

Figure 4.7. The voltage follower showing input resistances of the differential operational amplifier.

approaches equality with the input. In one sense nothing could be simpler, yet here one confronts feedback at its starkest. Note that curve c is the integral of b and that these curves everywhere satisfy the differential equation given in Figure 4.5. An intuitive grasp of the behavior of this circuit and an understanding of its differential equation are inseparable. Yet neither must necessarily come first and certainly the two are complementary. Curve b is the difference between curves a and c; curve c represents the area under b; curve b plots the slope of c. Perhaps those who found their first course in differential equations (". . . assume a solution of the form . . .") to be intellectually distressing may find solace in contemplation of the voltage follower. Nor should thoughts of retribution be entirely suppressed.

Although the foregoing is an accurate portrayal of the functioning of the follower, the speed of its response is so great that for many purposes its dynamic lag may be neglected. The time scale is indicated for a typical amplifier in Figure 4.6; the output has settled to within 0.01% of the final value within 1 microsecond. The assumption that the output replicates the input can usually be supported.

In Chapter 1 it was assumed that the input of the operational amplifier permitted no current flow. This assumption will now be supplanted by the circuit model in Figure 4.7, which is intended to be compared with Figure 4.2. The bootstrapped resistor R in Figure 4.2 corresponds with

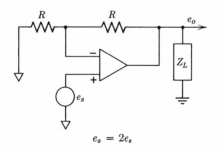

$$e_o = 2e_s$$

Figure 4.8.   Follower-with-gain of 2.

r_d in Figure 4.7; r_d represents the real resistance between the inputs of an actual differential amplifier. This resistance is called the differential-mode input resistance in the literature and on specification sheets. Thus follower action effectively removes r_d as a load on the source. The resistance r_{cm} is unaffected by the feedback; this is the common-mode input resistance, defined as the resistance from either input to ground. Fortunately, this resistance, which places the upper limit on follower input resistance, is typically greater than 1000 megohms in modern amplifiers. A follower with this input resistance makes a gain error of one part per thousand when connected to a 1-megohm signal source. Input resistances several orders of magnitude better can be had, but become insignificant compared with other sources of error.

A graphical treatment of the unity-gain follower degenerates to a point on a voltage-resistance plot. However, a direct descendant, the follower-with-gain of 2, is of major interest, both pedagogical and practical. Unlike the cathode follower, the operational follower is capable of gains greater than unity. Positive gains of more than 100 are perfectly practical, granted that the term *follower* is to be stretched to match the gain. In particular, the gain-of-2 circuit in Figure 4.8 is to be carefully compared with that in Figure 1.1. Observe that the input signal source is located differently; that is, the connections to the input resistor and to the direct input have been interchanged. Just as the single-ended amplifier maintains its input terminal at ground potential, so the differential amplifier maintains the potential *difference* between its inputs at zero volts. It can be seen that these statements are identical when the direct input of the differential amplifier is grounded. When it is

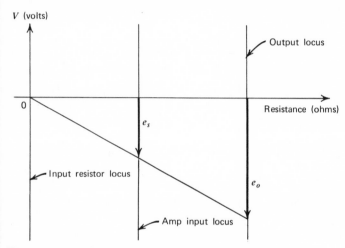

Figure 4.9.   Voltage-resistance plot for follower-with-gain of 2.

not grounded the feedback action causes the inverting input to be at the same voltage as the direct input. This principle is used to construct a voltage-resistance plot for the circuit of Figure 4.8; in Figure 4.9 the solution is given for a —1-volt source. The left-hand end of the input resistor is plotted at the origin since it is connected to ground or zero volts. A distance R ohms to the right is a vertical line representing the input-terminal locus. Because the signal source places the direct input at —1 volt the inverting input will also have this value. There are thus two points on a line as before, the slope of the line representing the current in the resistor. Again no current is presumed to flow in the input terminal. Accordingly the intersection of the inclined line with the vertical line of the output locus fixes the output voltage. It is twice

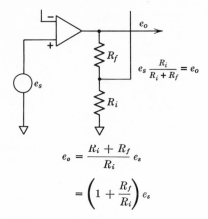

$$e_o = \frac{R_i + R_f}{R_i} e_s$$

$$= \left(1 + \frac{R_f}{R_i}\right) e_s$$

Figure 4.10.   The follower-with-gain as an activated voltage divider.

as great as the source and has the same sign. But of transcendent importance is the comparison of Figure 4.9 with Figure 1.5. It is not simply
that the figures can be made identical by shifting the ordinates—it is
that they represent what is *functionally the same circuit.*

Another point of view is that the resistor-to-ground and feedback
resistor are conceived as a voltage divider. The circuit is so redrawn
in Figure 4.10. The output is that voltage which when operated on by
the voltage divider is equal to the input voltage. A divider in the feedback path has the reciprocal effect on the forward path gain. The relevant algebra is given in Figure 4.10.

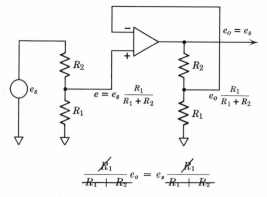

Figure 4.11.   The follower-with-gain viewed as the inverse of the simple voltage
divider.

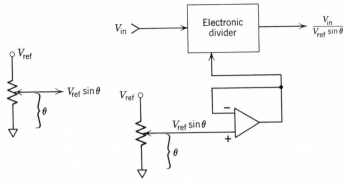

Figure 4.12. Division by the sine of a mechanical angle. (An ingenuous approach.)

Perhaps an even simpler viewpoint follows quickly from a mildly improper and therefore easily remembered aphorism—a differential amplifier with feedback treats its inputs as a nice young lady treats her knees—it keeps them together. Thus the output will always take on that value which keeps the inputs together in voltage. Accordingly the follower-with-gain may be conceptualized as in Figure 4.11. The intent is to show that the follower-with-gain undoes what the voltage divider does.

Brief reflection on Figure 4.11 dispels the novelty of the idea that a network in the feedback path has the opposite effect of the same network in the forward path. Yet even bigger fish lurk in these depths, because the principle holds for quite general networks, as exemplified below.

In a navigation system it was required to divide a voltage by the sine of a mechanical shaft angle. A standard nonlinear potentiometer

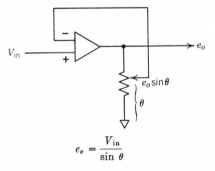

$$e_o = \frac{V_{in}}{\sin \theta}$$

Figure 4.13. Feedback to the rescue. (A highly disingenuous solution.)

giving an output voltage proportional to the sine of the shaft angle θ had been purchased. But because *division* by the sine function was needed it was thought that an electronic analog divider was required. That is, an arrangement such as that in Figure 4.12 was in prospect. Now when division by a *voltage* must be performed continuously an analog divider is essential. But that was not the case. The implementation in Figure 4.13 obviates the divider, the reference voltage source, and perhaps a follower amplifier, since the follower configuration inherently buffers the input signal source.

This example is drawn from practice; it is spectacular; it neatly emphasizes the reason for these writings.

Chapter V

Symmetric Circuitry

Invertor circuits change the sign of the signal; follower circuits do not. A third category combines the two and is seen in Figure 5.1 to be an outright celebration of the principle of symmetry. Appearances here are not deceiving—symmetry is the essence of this circuitry, the beauties of which are several and substantive. In particular, the circuit of Figure 5.1 enables the subtraction of large, nearly equal signals to yield an accurate difference. The difference amplifier, more than any other circuit, is fundamental to data-acquisition technology.

A combination of the invertor and the follower is best understood by superposition of these kinds of circuit action. First suppose that $e_2 = 0$ in Figure 5.1. The direct input is at zero volts because the am-

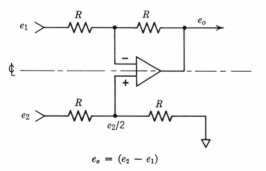

$$e_o = (e_2 - e_1)$$

Figure 5.1.   The difference amplifier. (Precise differential to single-ended converter.)

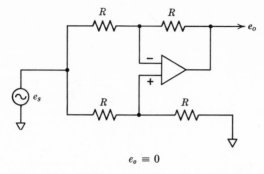

$$e_o \equiv 0$$

Figure 5.2. Difference-amplifier demonstration circuit.

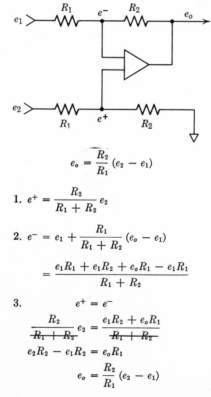

$$e_o = \frac{R_2}{R_1}(e_2 - e_1)$$

1. $e^+ = \dfrac{R_2}{R_1 + R_2} e_2$

2. $e^- = e_1 + \dfrac{R_1}{R_1 + R_2}(e_o - e_1)$

   $= \dfrac{e_1 R_1 + e_1 R_2 + e_o R_1 - e_1 R_1}{R_1 + R_2}$

3. $\qquad\qquad e^+ = e^-$

   $\dfrac{R_2}{\cancel{R_1 + R_2}} e_2 = \dfrac{e_1 R_2 + e_o R_1}{\cancel{R_1 + R_2}}$

   $e_2 R_2 - e_1 R_2 = e_o R_1$

   $\qquad e_o = \dfrac{R_2}{R_1}(e_2 - e_1)$

Figure 5.3. The difference amplifier with gain.

32

plifier draws no current at its input. Thus the configuration is the same as Figure 1.1 and the input e_1 is acted on by an invertor. Then suppose that $e_1 = 0$. One-half of e_2 appears at the direct $(+)$ input by action of the 2:1 voltage divider. The remainder of the circuit is simply a follower-with-gain of 2 (Figure 4.8). Hence e_2 is first divided by 2 and then multiplied by 2, finally appearing unchanged in amplitude and

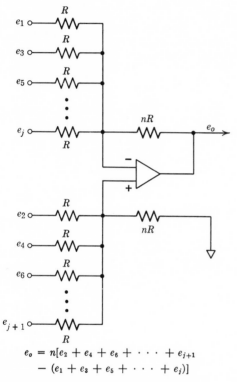

$$e_o = n[e_2 + e_4 + e_6 + \cdots + e_{j+1}$$
$$- (e_1 + e_3 + e_5 + \cdots + e_j)]$$

Figure 5.4.   Adder-subtractor with gain.

sign at the output. Since this is a linear circuit the superposition principle permits the addition of outputs due to the inputs separately to give the output for the inputs acting simultaneously.

Figure 5.2 sets forth a very important corollary property of the difference amplifier; if the inputs are tied together they may swing widely and rapidly in voltage without perturbing the output. This is as it should be because the circuit is supposed to register differences in input voltage, and if the inputs are tied together the difference is identically zero. This principle underlies test procedures for difference-amplifier circuits and for the differential operational amplifiers themselves. The action, or lack of action, is that the amplifier input terminals see a voltage

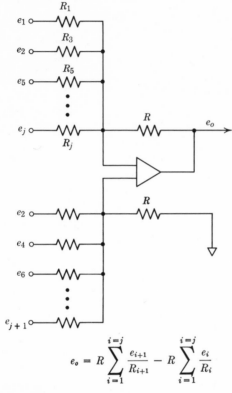

$$e_o = R \sum_{i=1}^{i=j} \frac{e_{i+1}}{R_{i+1}} - R \sum_{i=1}^{i=j} \frac{e_i}{R_i}$$

Symmetry condition:

$$\frac{1}{R_1} + \frac{1}{R_3} + \frac{1}{R_5} \cdots \frac{1}{R_j} = \frac{1}{R_2} + \frac{1}{R_4} + \frac{1}{R_6} \cdots + \frac{1}{R_{j+1}}$$

(number of inputs on each side need not be the same, but conductances must be equal)

Figure 5.5.   Weighted adder-subtractor with gain.

equal to one-half of the instantaneous source voltage, due to the two resistive voltage dividers. The output is at zero volts and stays that way because the differential input signal is forever zero. The circuit is said to reject the "common-mode" voltage of the input signals. That is, it does not respond to that part of the signal voltage which the inputs have in common; it registers only their difference. The difference of two inputs tied together is zero, and so is the output.

The circuit of Figure 5.1 subtracts two signals at unity gain. An equally good name for it is a double-ended to single-ended converter. It is used to transform a floating source into a grounded source for computation, filtering, nonlinear processing, or transmission.

The difference amplifier is not limited to unity gain. Symmetry is not violated if the feedback resistor and its mirror image are made different in value from the input resistors. See Figure 5.3 where the derivation of the performance equation is given with the proviso that it be ignored by all but the algebraically intrepid. It exploits the algebra of the voltage divider and the theorem that the differential inputs stay together. Note that the difference amplifier with gain less than unity is of particular practical importance. Given appropriately rated input resistors it can be used to measure small voltage differences between, for example, two power lines operating at *thousands* of volts ac or dc, because the differential character of the circuit holds up into the audio range of frequencies. Of course, this kind of measurement is not undertaken casually, but given careful circuit engineering it is eminently practical.

Multiple input symmetric circuits are called Adder-Subtractor circuits. If differential operational amplifiers are used these configurations offer a saving in amplifier count. It must be emphasized that symmetry is a *sine qua non* for these circuits; when it is violated the response equations lose their simple form. Fortunately, the required symmetry conditions are easily met. Figure 5.4 exhibits the adder-subtractor with gain. The simplest approach to the symmetry requirement is to make the number of inputs the same on each side and to ground unused inputs. Figure 5.5 shows the adder-subtractor in its most general form, together with the symmetry condition which must be satisfied.

Signals may be subtracted using only single-ended amplifier circuits; general-purpose analog computers are a case in point. The invert-and-add algorithm remains serviceable and is much used; yet the attractions of the symmetric circuit configuration are substantial and often subtle, and will be pointed out in connection with the special circuits that exploit them.

Chapter VI

Precise Diode Circuitry

All the circuitry discussed thus far has been linear circuitry. The peculiar power of operational circuitry derives from the ease with which nonlinear and linear operations can be combined. This chapter introduces diode circuits and shows how they can be arranged to perform important tasks with precision. The rationale of these undertakings is that the contriving of contrivances is a game for all—now the rewards of electronic cleverness begin to be revealed.

Diode circuits abound in the literature; most are approximate because diodes are not ideal. The circuits in this chapter are precise by virtue of the way the amplifier is used to extract ideal performance from the diodes. *The technique is crucial to sound nonlinear design.*

The simplest diode circuit has the same response as the ideal diode shown in Figure 6.1. It blocks signals of one polarity and transmits perfectly those of the other. Thus the circuit of Figure 6.2 emulates the response of a perfect half-wave rectifier (except for the gratuitous inversion). Figures 6.3 to 6.5 delineate the nonideal character of the silicon diode: (1) there is an effective voltage offset that varies from diode to diode and which is a strong function of temperature. (2) The diode has a logarithmic volt-ampere characteristic, giving it a nonzero and variable resistance when conducting. Both imperfections are overcome by feedback in the circuitry below.

Returning to Figure 6.2: when the input signal is negative the output swings positive. Diode D_1 blocks and D_2 conducts, driving the load and the feedback resistor. The feedback loop is thus closed around diode

D_2, and the high voltage gain of the amplifier ensures that the output voltage, e_A, in Figure 6.2 is sufficient to provide the circuit output voltage, e_o, plus the voltage drop across diode D_2. That is, the action is the same as in a simple invertor. The voltage at the summing point is microscopically larger than if diode D_2 were absent. Note that the size

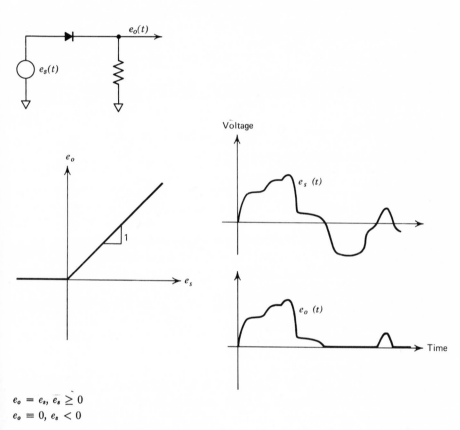

$e_o = e_s, \; e_s \geq 0$
$e_o \equiv 0, \; e_s < 0$

Figure 6.1. Response of the ideal diode.

of the voltage drop across the diode is immaterial, as are its variations with temperature and time. Because the diode is inside the feedback loop, with the high gain of the amplifier preceding it, its vagaries are reduced to irrelevance; they are said to be "servo-ed out" by the high-gain loop.

When the input signal becomes more positive than zero, so (minutely) does the summing point voltage, causing the amplifier output to swing negative. Diode D_2 blocks and D_1 conducts. The output swings sufficiently negative to draw off through D_1 all current delivered to the summing point by the input resistor, thus keeping the summing point

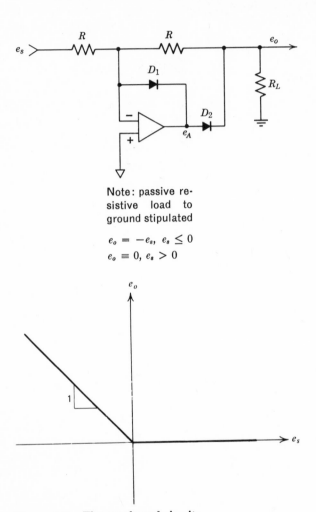

Note: passive resistive load to ground stipulated

$$e_o = -e_s, \ e_s \le 0$$
$$e_o \equiv 0, \ e_s > 0$$

Figure 6.2. The zero-bound circuit.

at virtual ground. Because the load is passive (contains no energy sources) and is purely resistive (contains no stored energy), the output voltage is zero. Diode D_2, which is blocking, has an effective resistance of thousands of megohms and may be ignored.

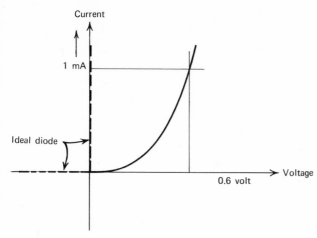

Figure 6.3. Volt-ampere characteristic of typical silicon diode.

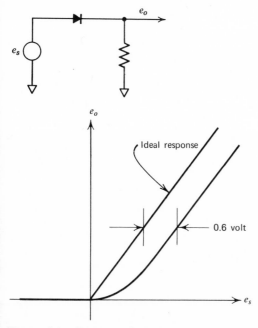

Figure 6.4. Response of simple rectifier circuit.

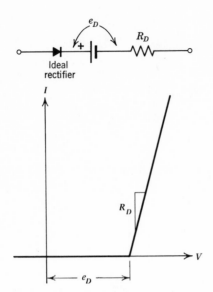

Figure 6.5. Circuit model representing silicon diode.

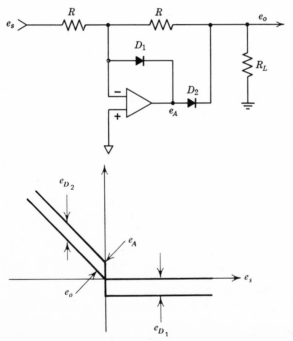

Figure 6.6. Principle of the activated diode circuit.

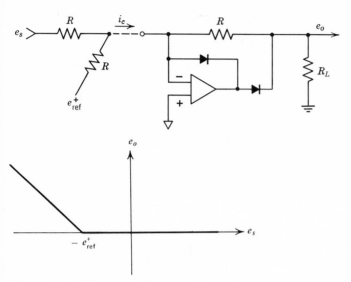

Figure 6.7. The current-biased zero-bound circuit.

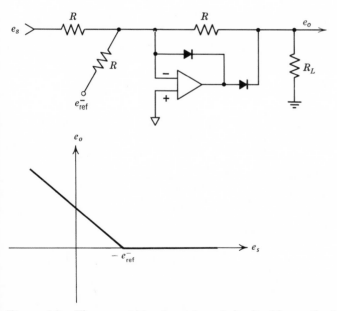

Figure 6.8. The current-biased zero-bound circuit with negative bias voltage.

By way of graphical recapitulation, Figure 6.6 shows the amplifier output voltage as well as the circuit output voltage.

The zero-bound circuit gets its name because the output voltage is constrained to precisely zero when the signal is of the polarity to be rejected. But the name should not be construed to imply that the inflection point is restricted to zero-volts input signal. A simple biasing scheme enables the inflection point to be placed anywhere on the input signal range, positive or negative. Figure 6.7 shows the scheme in a slightly

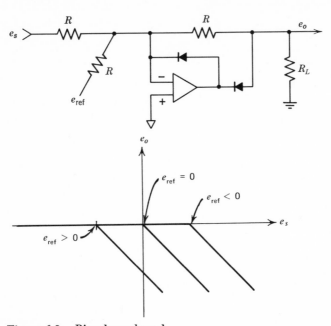

Figure 6.9.   Biased zero-bound.

exploded form. The essence of it is that the sign of the summing point voltage controls which mode the circuit is in. This voltage in turn depends on whether signal current is flowing toward or away from the summing point; this current is labeled i_c in Figure 6.7. It will flow in the direction of the arrow unless the input signal is negative and greater in magnitude than the positive reference voltage. When the input signal exceeds this negative value the current i_c reverses and the output inflection point occurs. The response of the same circuit with a negative reference voltage is shown in Figure 6.8. In Figure 6.9 the result of reversing the diodes is shown for various values of the reference voltage.

Note that the biasing quantity is really a current in Figures 6.7 to 6.9. For simplicity of presentation the bias resistor was chosen equal to the input resistor, thus allowing the bias voltage to be plotted on the input signal axis directly. But in general, wide latitude exists in the biasing arrangement. It is often convenient to use one of the regulated

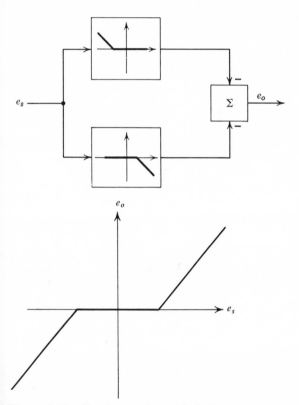

Figure 6.10.   Dead-space circuit block diagram.

power supply voltages as the bias energy source, and to choose the bias resistor value accordingly. Sometimes the inflection point is not fixed but is a variable set by a voltage signal elsewhere in the system. This voltage signal, which will be an amplifier output or other low-impedance source, is connected to the bias resistor, the value of which is chosen to relate the two signals properly. In simple terms, the ratio of the bias resistor to the input resistor is the same as the ratio of the bias

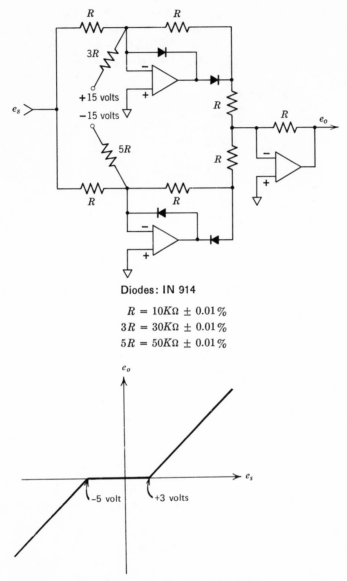

Diodes: IN 914

$$R = 10K\Omega \pm 0.01\%$$
$$3R = 30K\Omega \pm 0.01\%$$
$$5R = 50K\Omega \pm 0.01\%$$

Figure 6.11. Dead-space circuit schematic diagram.

voltage to the input signal voltage at which the inflection point is to occur. That is, a bias current is connected of such a value that the current i_c changes direction at the desired value of the input signal. A rereading of this extended explanation is justified by the power of the technique.

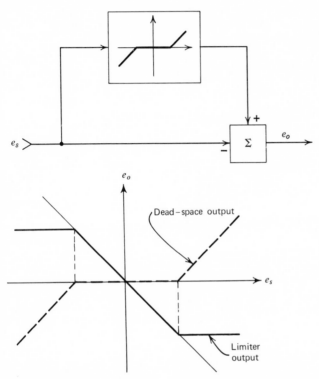

Figure 6.12.   Limiter circuit by subtraction of dead-space function from the signal.

A dead-zone or dead-space circuit is often required. The outputs of two suitably biased zero-bound circuits may be added to give this function. Figure 6.10 illustrates this circuit in block diagram form, and Figure 6.11 shows a practical schematic. The deadspace has been made unsymmetrical by the choice of bias resistors. Notice that there is no overall signal inversion because of the second inversion at the summing amplifier. This second inversion corresponds with the minus signs on the summation block in Figure 6.10.

Precise circuits to implement a saturation characteristic are not easy to devise; these circuits are called limiters or clippers. They are closely related to the deadband circuit and can be derived from it by subtraction. Figure 6.12 shows the block diagram and the input-output plot. In Figure 6.13 it is seen that the clipper circuit evolves from the deadspace circuit by the addition of a single resistor—an especially appealing outcome.

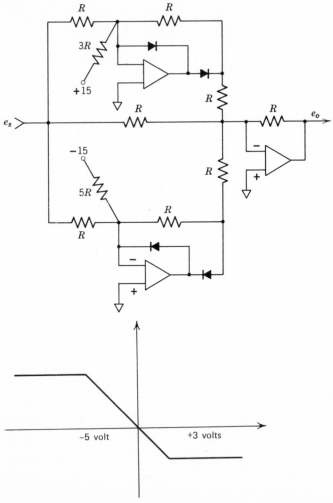

Figure 6.13. Limiter circuit schematic.

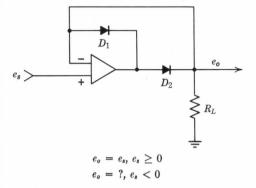

$$e_o = e_s, \; e_s \geq 0$$
$$e_o = ?, \; e_s < 0$$

Figure 6.14.   Attempt at positive-gain activated diode circuit.

Figure 6.13, like Figure 6.11, has an asymmetrical response. Both circuits are usually made symmetric.

The zero-bound circuit of Figure 6.2 is related to the unity-gain invertor; an analogous circuit based on the follower might appear as in Figure 6.14, promising a zero-bound without the inversion. Simplistic reasoning by analogy is known to have its pitfalls and this is a case in point, although not without redeeming tutorial value. Diode D_2 functions just as does its counterpart in the inverting circuit and has a loop closed around it in the same way. However, D_1 behaves less fortunately. When the input signal is negative, D_1 conducts and closes the loop, thus keeping the amplifier from saturating and obviating error during recovery from saturation. But D_1 also drags the circuit output negative along with it. The circuit is redrawn in Figure 6.15 to make the action unmistakeable. In fact, the high-gain amplifier preceding the diodes activates both of them—idealizing the pair of diodes so that

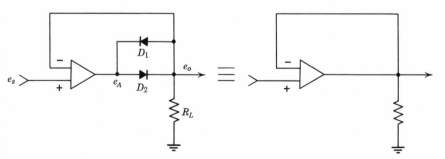

Figure 6.15.   Figure 6.14 redrawn.

it resembles nothing so much as a piece of wire! That is, the circuit acts like a simple follower. This behavior is instructive if apparently useless. It is diagrammed in Figure 6.16. The amplifier output voltage jumps *accurately at the zero crossing* of the input signal, thus servoing out the diode drops so that the circuit output voltage replicates the input. Here is an example of a frequent occurrence in circuit manipulation: today's fiasco, properly understood and exploited, becomes tomor-

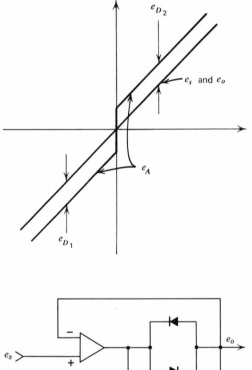

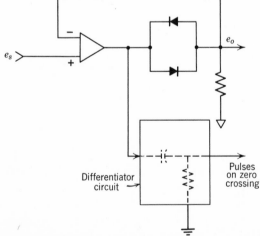

Figure 6.16.   The anatomy of a fiasco, somewhat recouped by a saving grace.

row's useful new circuit. In this case the connection of a differentiator circuit (perhaps as simple as the RC network indicated) to the amplifier output terminal generates a pulse output whenever zero crossings of the input occur—the polarity of the pulse indicating the direction of the crossing. In addition, the high-input impedance, accurate unity gain, and load-driving ability of the voltage follower are retained.

The foregoing, whatever its pedagogic and practical utility, remains a digression. The main business is the quest for a positive-gain ideal diode circuit—a circuit having the response shown in Figure 6.17. A principal motive should become clear from Figure 6.18: such a circuit leads to a precise absolute value circuit, which is big game indeed.

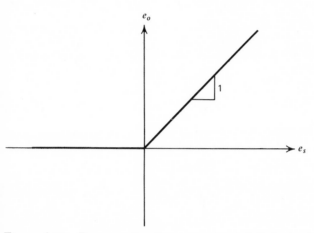

Figure 6.17.   Response of positive-gain activated diode circuit.

The much maligned circuit of Figure 6.14 can be salvaged by the addition of two inexpensive resistors. It remains a circuit fragment, not to be used alone, as hinted by the dashed line in Figure 6.19, and then only with grounded passive loads. The $10K$-ohm resistor prevents the amplifier output from being directly connected to the circuit output when D_1 conducts; the resistor does not interfere with accurate feedback while D_2 is conducting. The resistor in series with the direct input has a temperature compensation function which is secondary and will be treated in the chapter on amplifier errors.

The final absolute-value-circuit schematic appears in Figure 6.20. It is noteworthy in that its accuracy depends only on the precision of the match between the resistors R in the zero-bound circuit. It is required

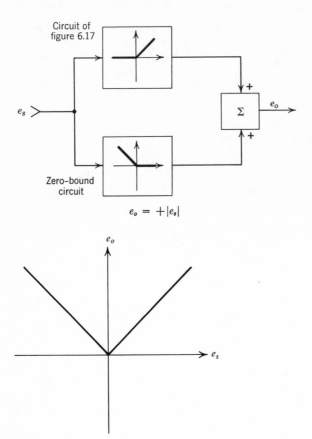

$$e_o = +|e_s|$$

Figure 6.18. Block diagram of precise absolute value circuit.

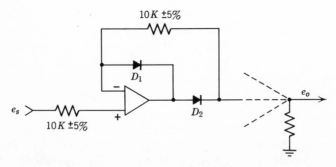

Figure 6.19. Positive-gain activated diode-circuit fragment.

50

only that these are a matched pair (and that their time and temperature stability be such that they *stay* that way); the accuracy of their ohmic value is immaterial. It is also of interest that the outputs are summed simply by being connected in parallel. The amplifier that is active drives the load accurately under the control of its own feedback loop.

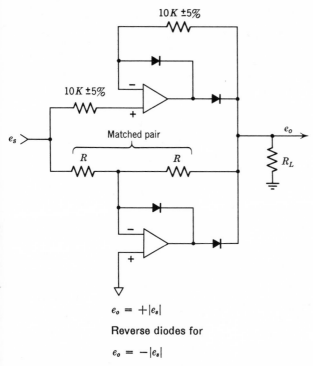

$$e_o = +|e_s|$$

Reverse diodes for

$$e_o = -|e_s|$$

Figure 6.20.   Absolute value circuit.

The same approach yields a precise selector circuit. This circuit, shown as an upper selector in Figure 6.21, delivers at its output the most positive (or least negative) of its several input voltages. A lower selector results when the diodes are reversed and the bias voltage inverted. The output of the upper selector is called the upper bound of its input ensemble; that of the lower selector is called the lower bound. The circuit comprises any number of the circuit fragments of Figure 6.19, with their outputs common. The circuit fragment that has the most positive input will have its D_2 diode switched on and will inflict its input signal on

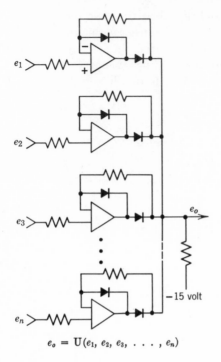

$$e_o = U(e_1, e_2, e_3, \ldots, e_n)$$

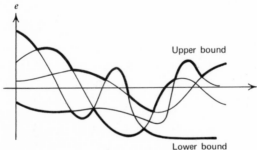

Figure 6.21. Upper-voltage selector circuit.

the circuit output by precise follower action. The other amplifiers will be bounded by conduction of their respective D_1 diodes.

Precise selection opens a whole area of maximum-minimum mathematics to easy circuit implementation.

A peak-follower circuit is closely related in form and function. A precise circuit is shown in Figure 6.22, along with a time history of its performance after a reset has been given. Reversing the diodes causes

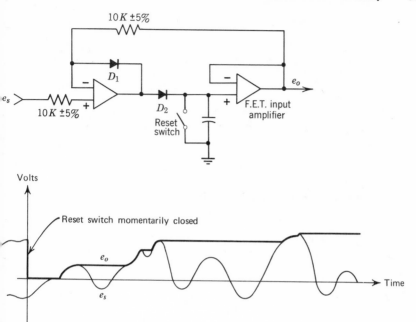

Figure 6.22.   Peak follower circuit.

negative peaks or valleys to be followed and held. The reset switch
may be manual or mechanized; some of the more artful examples in
the chapter on system synthesis involve automatic actuation of this
switch.

All the circuits in this chapter are the best of the breed. As noted
earlier there is a wide range of simpler circuits with correspondingly
modest performance. Three arguments support the circuits of this chapter; the circuits are

(1) illustrative of feedback technique,

(2) conservative of the dynamic range of 10-volt operational circuitry,
and

(3) indicative of the changed economics of circuit design—an amplifier
costs about the same as a precision resistor as of January 1971.

Chapter VII

Wheatstone Bridge Circuitry

Electrical instrumentation may be taken to have begun with this famous circuit configuration; direct descendents of Wheatstone's bridge are the basis of the modern electrical standards laboratory. Many instruments in use today are basically self-balancing bridges. But this chapter is not concerned with balanced bridges; rather the topic is operational circuits that linearly convert bridge unbalance to voltage. The typical sensor or transducer exhibits a change of resistance in response to the measured physical quantity; devices as various as the cadmium sulfide photoresistor, the resistance strain gage, and the platinum resistance thermometer come immediately to mind. Circuits for converting the resistance changes of these and similar devices into voltage signals—linearly and without moving parts—are important to all the cybernetic pursuits. Not only are voltage signals convenient for meters, indicators, and recorders; equally important is their suitability as command or response signals in systems. It is in this latter role that a premium is placed on linearity. If only point-by-point measurements are taken a curvilinear response from an instrument becomes incorporated in its calibration curve and is not a great embarassment; but increasingly instrument outputs become part of the data stream of real-time systems where linearity, reliability, and (sometimes) speed are essential.

An ordinary Wheatstone bridge is distressingly nonlinear, even for small percentage unbalances. A rough rule is that a $p\%$ unbalanced

ridge suffers an output voltage "droop" or linearity error of $\frac{1}{2}p\%$—
hen the bridge voltage is measured with a high-resistance amplifier
s in Figure 7.1. Low-impedance meters cause linearity errors twice as
reat, the error being a function of metering circuit resistance. It is
ir to state that unbalanced bridges from the algebraic, conceptual,
nd practical standpoints are rather a mess. If only one arm of the
ridge is varying, it can be placed in a differential amplifier circuit,
nd the voltage readout is absolutely linear. But if more than one arm
s an active transducer the conventional diamond-shaped bridge is in
erious trouble. Ironically, recent semiconductor transducers offer very
igh sensitivities in terms of change of resistance per unit of physical
nput; this ordinarily welcome sensitivity exacerbates the problem of
ne nonlinear response of conventional bridges.

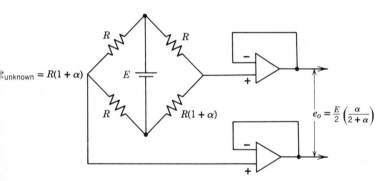

igure 7.1.   Conventional Wheatstone bridge.

A special mechanical arrangement of the gages imparts linearity to
he response of the multitude of strain-gage transducers for force, pres-
ure, acceleration, et cetera; in these devices an increment in the resis-
ance of a gage is accompanied by an equal decrement in its series
nate. The result is a series combination of constant resistance and hence
onstant current under voltage excitation; linear resistance to voltage
onversion may easily be shown to follow. Upon this one artifice has
ested a large part of modern instrumentation.

Since bridges are a means to the end of measuring resistance and
onductance, and sums and differences of resistances and conductances,
review of the definitions of these parameters is in order. In Figure
.2 resistance is defined in terms of the voltage a known dc current
ets up in passing through the unknown element. Similarly, in the same
gure conductance is defined by the current that passes through an

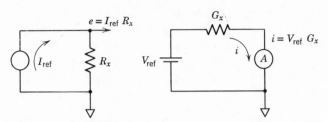

Figure 7.2.   Ideal resistance and conductance readout circuits.

unknown element subjected to a known dc terminal voltage. It is implicit that the voltage measurement be made with an instrument that draws no current, and that the current be measured with an instrument that has zero voltage across its terminals. These conditions obtain in the circuits below.

The circuits of this chapter are variations of the active Ohm's law circuit of Figure 7.3. Two properties are salient:

1. The output voltage depends only on the product of resistance and current.

2. The inverting input voltage is zero.

This configuration is often presented as a zero voltage drop or zero-resistance current-meter circuit. That is, it serves the same function as an ammeter or milliammeter one terminal of which is grounded, and it does so ideally by allowing no voltage drop across the terminals. (For comparison, a moving-coil meter with 1-milliampere full-scale sensitivity typically has 100-ohms internal resistance. Thus 1 milliampere

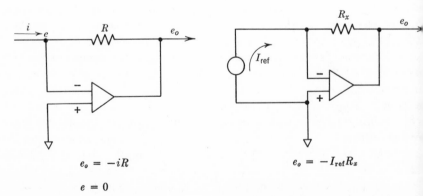

Figure 7.3.   Underlying principle.   **Figure 7.4.**   Resistance readout.

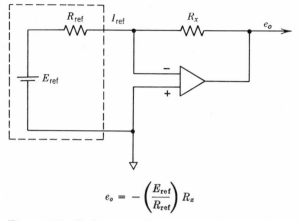

$$e_o = - \left(\frac{E_{ref}}{R_{ref}} \right) R_x$$

Figure 7.5. Resistance readout.

is measured at the cost of a 100-millivolt intrusion upon the measured circuit, which may be a catastrophic disruption.) The conductance read-out schemes in this chapter make use of this current-measuring property. Resistance is measured by placing the unknown element in the feedback path and connecting a known current source, as seen in Figure 7.4. The second circuit property makes the construction of a reference current source almost trivial. Because the current is to be driven into a terminal whose voltage never varies from zero, a grounded voltage reference and a known resistor serve perfectly. See Figure 7.5 which is similar to Figure 2.6. The related scheme for conductance readout uses the same hardware and the same principles, but with both rearranged. See Figure 7.6. Because the amplifier keeps its inverting input at zero volts, the total reference voltage is impressed across the unknown conductance; the active Ohm's law circuit is used to read out the resulting current. A consistent attitude toward these techniques is difficult to maintain, the more

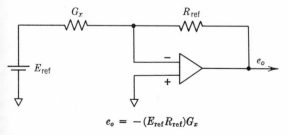

$$e_o = - (E_{ref} R_{ref}) G_x$$

Figure 7.6. Conductance readout.

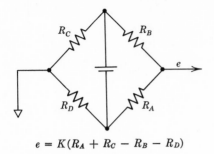

$$e = K(R_A + R_C - R_B - R_D)$$

Figure 7.7. Ideal bridge response.

so as they become thoroughly understood; it is not clear whether they are trivial or profound, self-evident or monumental.

The topological arrangement of the Wheatstone bridge makes it inherently an adder and subtractor of resistances and conductances. The subtractive property in particular is responsible for the preeminence of the bridge in high-resolution comparison arrangements; that is, it is adapted to the detection of small differences. The response of an idealized bridge is given in Figure 7.7. This is the response of a real bridge for small perturbations from the balanced condition; below are circuits having this characteristic for *any* degree of unbalance.

Figure 7.8 comprises the resistance readout circuit of Figure 7.5 used twice. It applies the idea that resistances can be added by connecting

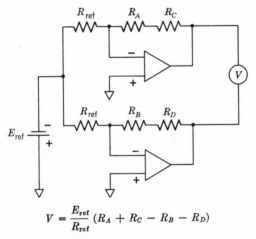

$$V = \frac{E_{ref}}{R_{ref}} (R_A + R_C - R_B - R_D)$$

Figure 7.8. Bridge-surrogate circuit. (Linear for all unbalanced conditions.)

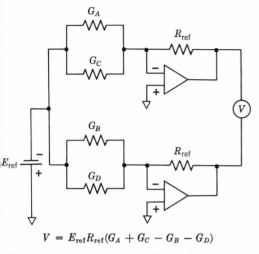

$$V = E_{\text{ref}}R_{\text{ref}}(G_A + G_C - G_B - G_D)$$

Figure 7.9. Conductance bridge-surrogate circuit.

them in series, hardly a radical departure. The subtractive function is performed by the floating meter, a task for which even the digital volt-meters are well suited. Figure 7.9 is the same trick based on Figure 7.6. Conductances are added by connecting them in parallel, not so obvious but equally sound.

When it is necessary to develop the bridge output as a single-ended

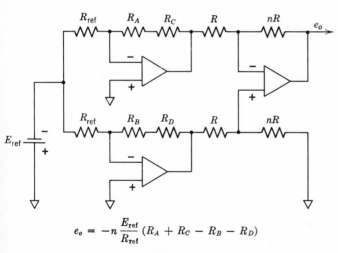

$$e_o = -n \frac{E_{\text{ref}}}{R_{\text{ref}}} (R_A + R_C - R_B - R_D)$$

Figure 7.10. Figure 7.8 with difference amplifier with gain.

signal referenced to ground potential, additional hardware and artfulness are required. A difference amplifier is a standard approach for both circuits; the difference amplifier with gain allows amplification, which may well be needed. See Figures 7.10 and 7.11. Objections are that a differential amplifier and pairs of matched resistors are required, and that the gain is not easily changed. A further objection is raised by the circuit purist who feels the heavy hand of brute force at work. This almost aesthetic invocation of economy of means has merit, at least in retrospect. An amplifier must still be added to the circuit of Figure 7.8, but it can be a single-ended type if the voltage reference can be floated, as it possibly can if it serves only the one circuit. A

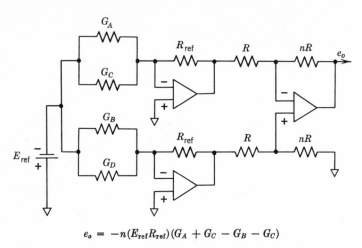

$$e_o = -n(E_{ref}R_{ref})(G_A + G_C - G_B - G_C)$$

Figure 7.11.   Figure 7.9 with difference amplifier with gain.

single-ended amplifier is important if chopper-stabilized amplifiers are required, because only single-ended amplifiers are available in the stabilized types. The resulting circuit appears in Figure 7.12; it saves a reference resistor and provides a convenient gain adjustment. Note that the current in all four "bridge" resistors is equal by identity.

Similar treatment cannot be applied to Figure 7.9 because the source cannot be floated to achieve the effective subtraction. However, another opportunity appears. See Figure 7.13. The two resistors R need only be matched, their value being immaterial. The lower amplifier functions as a current invertor. Note that R_{ref} may be chosen to give the required gain, or may be made adjustable as in the preceding case.

Since these circuits respond linearly to sums and differences of the

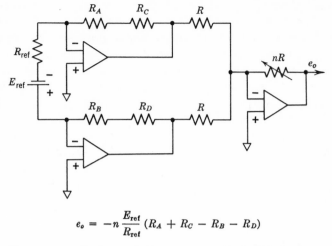

$$e_o = -n \frac{E_{ref}}{R_{ref}} (R_A + R_C - R_B - R_D)$$

Figure 7.12. Resistance bridge-surrogate circuit with floating source and simplified output.

total values of the elements, they inherently give linear response to *deviations*, that is, to increments or decrements from nominal values. Note that the number of elements is not limited to four, and that the linearity property makes precise summation or averaging a simple matter.

It was remarked above that a single element can be read out linearly

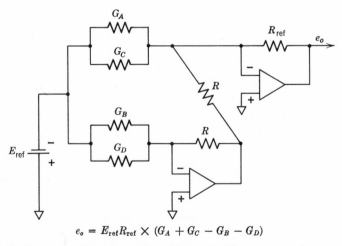

$$e_o = E_{ref}R_{ref} \times (G_A + G_C - G_B - G_D)$$

Figure 7.13. Final form of conductance bridge-surrogate circuit.

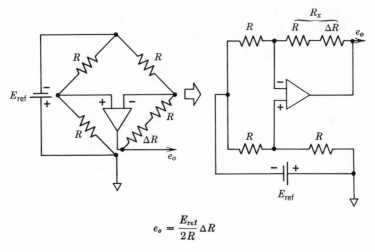

$$e_o = \frac{E_{ref}}{2R} \Delta R$$

Figure 7.14.   Resistance deviation readout by differential amplifier.

with a differential amplifier circuit. In this case it is the deviation from the nominal value that is of interest, rather than the total value of the element; more pointedly, the total value is a decided nuisance when high-resolution measurement of small changes in it is the objective. This is a fair statement of what is called the zero-suppression problem—it is *the* problem that the classical bridge circuit dispatched. Figure 7.14 illustrates the principle of the differential linear readout circuit, and shows how the circuit is related to the traditional bridge. The resistive deviation is drawn as a separate resistor in series with the nominal value, even though both are physically the same element; it is understood

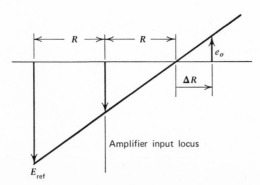

Figure 7.15.   Voltage-resistance plot for circuit of Figure 7.14.

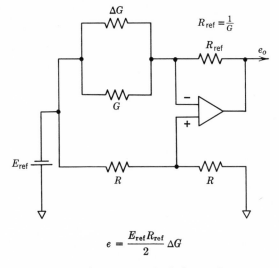

$$e = \frac{E_{ref} R_{ref}}{2} \Delta G$$

Figure 7.16. Conductance deviation readout.

that, for example, a negative value of ΔR represents a decrease in the total resistance from the nominal value. The voltage at the amplifier inputs is set at one-half of the reference voltage by the voltage divider connected to the direct input. The current through R_x is thus fixed. If ΔR is zero, so is the output voltage; positive and negative output voltages are proportional to corresponding values of ΔR. The output voltage takes on the value that is needed to satisfy Ohm's law across R_x, as the voltage-resistance graph of Figure 7.15 should help to make clear.

The corresponding circuit for conductance deviation is given in Figure 7.16. Although both of these circuits work well, they should be considered primarily illustrative; refined versions are given in the chapter on instrumentation (Chapter 11), where they exemplify the extraction of the ultimate performance from a given amplifier type.

Chapter VIII

Voltage- and Current-Meter Circuitry

Meters provide visual readout of electrical quantities. Among the many types are moving pointers, oscilloscopes, strip-chart recorders, X-Y plotters, digital displays, numerical printers, et cetera. Whatever the form or format, the result is conversion of an electrical quantity into a readable form.

Meter circuits are noteworthy for what they do *not* do—they do not disturb the quantity measured. This function is assigned to the first block of Figure 8.1. All meter circuits can be anatomized into the form of this figure, although some of the more interesting circuits achieve economy by an intimate mixture of the hardware that performs the two functions.

The division of function is perfectly plain in the volt-meter circuit of Figure 8.2. This figure is comprehensive of all cases where the readout device is an existing voltage-sensitive instrument, one input terminal of which must be grounded. The operational follower simply unloads

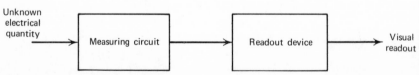

Figure 8.1. Generic meter circuit.

or buffers the measured circuit by virtue of its superlative input resistance (typically 1000 megohms). A follower-with-gain may be used to amplify the measured voltage.

A more instructive situation arises in the construction of a voltmeter "from scratch" using a moving-coil meter. These meters are simple, rugged, small, and relatively inexpensive; their accuracy and resolution are limited to about 1% of full scale, which means that their use sacrifices at least two orders of magnitude of the accuracy attainable with operational circuitry. Nevertheless, circuits built around these meters are appropriate to a large class of measurements. Furthermore, their simplicity and inherent electrical isolation make possible sophisticated measurements with very simple hardware.

A moving-coil current meter is basically a galvanometer with a graduated scale; it is current sensitive in that pointer deflection is proportional to the current flowing. A meter that has a sensitivity of 100 microamperes

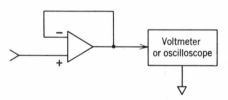

Figure 8.2. Ideal single-ended dc voltmeter.

for full-scale deflection is adequate for operational circuits. More sensitive meter movements are available, but sensitivity and fragility are necessarily related. The 0.1-milliampere movement is rugged enough for portable instruments.

An ideal meter for current has zero resistance; the moving coil of the real microammeter in question has about 1000 ohms due to the resistance of the fine copper windings. Moreover, the resistance of copper, like that of most metals, is strongly temperature-dependent. The few alloys that have nearly zero temperature coefficient of resistance are used in resistors for stability. It is thus incumbent upon the designer to insure that the current through a meter depends not on its own resistance but on that of stable resistors elsewhere in the circuit. A traditional approach called "swamping" is shown in Figure 8.3. A large stable resistor R is placed in series with the meter. If 10 volts are to produce 100 microamperes through a 1000-ohm winding, a 99,000-ohm series resistor is called for. It is evident that the temperature dependence of the winding has been "swamped-out" by a factor of 99.

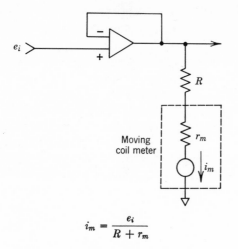

$$i_m = \frac{e_i}{R + r_m}$$

Figure 8.3.   High-resistance voltmeter.

Two objections apply to the above procedure: (1) 99,000 is a much less convenient value than 100,000, and (2) accurate meter current is achieved at the cost of 100 times more voltage across the meter-scaling-resistor combination than across the meter itself. This is not onerous in the case of a 10-volt full-scale voltmeter, but is quite impossible in other instances, for example, a portable instrument operated from 2.7-volt mercury batteries. Both objections are met by the circuit shown in Figure 8.4. Because the meter is in the feedback path, the current through it is predetermined and is *independent* of its own resistance. The amplifier pumps current into the grounded resistor R in order to

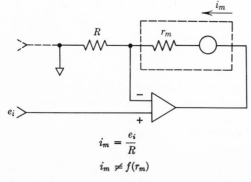

$$i_m = \frac{e_i}{R}$$

$$i_m \neq f(r_m)$$

Figure 8.4.   Improved high-resistance voltmeter.

make the voltage at the negative input follow the voltage at the positive input; this current must flow through the meter. It is Ohm's law again in a slightly different guise. The amplifier input retains the high resistance of the simple follower; note however that the output voltage is not to be trusted.

These matters are dramatized in Figure 8.5. Even a voltage source in series with the meter is powerless to influence the current through it. An equally impotent nonlinear resistor is also shown in series. The meter current is precisely related to the input voltage alone. The only proviso is that the amplifier must have sufficient output-voltage capability (called voltage swing) to equal the input voltage plus the worst case sum of the voltages across the "garbage" in the loop. Again, as

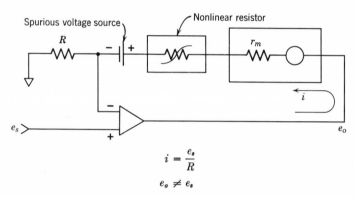

$$i = \frac{e_s}{R}$$

$$e_o \neq e_s$$

Figure 8.5. Demonstration of properties of circuit of Figure 8.4.

indicated in Figure 8.5, the amplifier's output voltage is no longer simply related to the input voltage; it is said to "servo around" to accommodate the meter voltage and the other extraneous voltages in the loop so that the *current* is correct. The gratuitous voltage source and nonlinear resistor are, of course, not added purposely in a practical case. However, they do fairly represent the behavior of real diodes used in the ac meter circuits to come. If it is required to monitor a voltage and to send it elsewhere as a signal, Figure 8.3 must be used; for the pure metering function Figure 8.4 is preferable.

The circuits discussed so far measure voltage with respect to ground or zero potential. On the other hand, a simple voltmeter is inherently differential. The simple meter consists of a galvanometer and a series resistor; the current that flows and hence the meter deflection depend only on the voltage *difference* across which the meter is connected. A high-resistance version of the simple voltmeter is made by prefacing it with two operational followers as in Figure 8.6. This circuit is a differential form of Figure 8.3 and shares its disadvantages. Figure 8.7 is the differential form of the improved circuit of Figure 8.4. Note the high sensitivity available in the improved circuits by simply making R small. Furthermore notice the ease of scale changing by switching the value of R; that is, because the meter resistance does not enter the scaling equation, gain setting is very straightforward. In Figure 8.7,

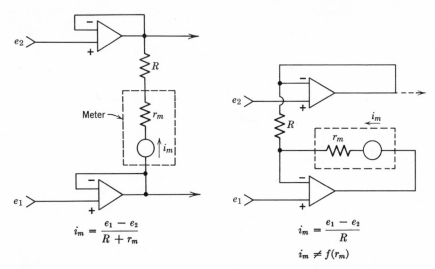

$$i_m = \frac{e_1 - e_2}{R + r_m}$$

$$i_m = \frac{e_1 - e_2}{R}$$

$$i_m \neq f(r_m)$$

Figure 8.6. High-resistance differential voltmeter.

Figure 8.7. Improved high-resistance differential voltmeter.

input e_2 appears unadulterated and at low impedance at the output of the upper follower; its further use as a signal is legitimate.

Given an amplifier with its own floating power supply (a battery-powered amplifier for example) it is no trick to build floating meters. Figure 8.8 is a battery version of Figure 8.4; the instrument floats because the power supply does; it is capable of measuring voltage differences of up to the amplifier's rated swing as a follower with the given supply voltages. For example, a circuit powered by ± 2.7-volt batteries can typically measure ± 1 volt. (A special amplifier type is used for the very low voltage given in the example.) The input impedance is that of a conventional follower.

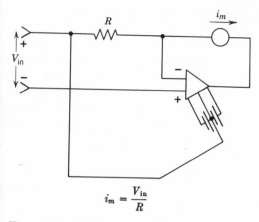

$$i_m = \frac{V_{in}}{R}$$

Figure 8.8.   Battery-powered floating differential voltmeter.

The discussion thus far has dealt with voltmeters; the measurement of current owes even more to operational technique. Consider the 100-microampere, 1000-ohm meter movement cited above, which is typical high-quality industrial hardware. In measuring the current of an unknown source that has an internal resistance of 100,000 ohms or less, this meter, by its 1000-ohm intrusion, causes an error of 1% or more. The problem is diagrammed in Figure 8.9. To measure a current means to measure it under *short-circuit* conditions, just as voltage measurement implies open-circuit conditions. That is, just as a voltmeter should have very high resistance so as not to draw current from the measured circuit, just so an ammeter should have very low resistance so as not to intrude a voltage drop of its own into the current loop it measures. If the unknown source in Figure 8.9 had comprised 1 volt and 10,000 ohms to give the 100 microamperes, a 10% error would have been caused by

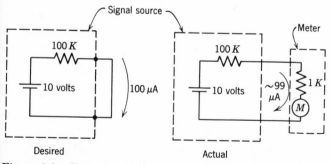

Figure 8.9.   Error caused by nonzero resistance of current meter.

the meter. As the source resistance falls even lower, one enters a realm that must be called estimate rather than measurement.

The operational amplifier brings to the rescue its ultrasensitive inputs for sensing the unknown and the ample power of its output for driving the meter. Since the basic difficulty was that the energy to deflect the meter was drawn from the item being measured, interposing the amplifier corrects the situation. Uncertainties remain but are orders of magnitude smaller. These uncertainties are characteristics of the amplifier and are treated in the chapter on that subject (Chapter 9).

Figure 8.10 reveals the principle underlying current measurement with the operational amplifier; it is the current-to-voltage converter that should now be familiar to the reader. The crucial point is that the current measurement is made under almost perfect short-circuit conditions. The virtual ground of the fedback amplifier input is presented to the un-

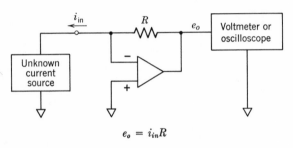

$$e_o = i_{in}R$$

Figure 8.10.   Zero-drop current-meter circuit.

known—which is presumed to be grounded in this example. Thus even with the most prosaic amplifier the voltage disturbance will be less than 1 millivolt, even for a 10-volt output to the readout device. An oscilloscope is shown in this latter role because often the phenomenon to be measured is a dynamic one, as for example in biological systems. A photograph of an oscilloscope trace can be scaled to respectable accuracy (1 or 2%), although most often it is the shape rather than the size of the signal that is of interest. Note that an improper meter circuit may so disturb the system that the character of the response is altered; biological systems are again a case in point.

Figure 8.11 presents the simplest zero-drop current-measurement circuit. The circuit action should now be evident. This circuit has been called a current follower. From a circuit theory standpoint it is the exact "dual" of the voltage follower. It is restricted to measuring currents

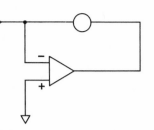

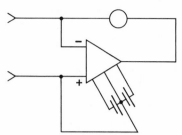

Figure 8.11. Direct reading zero-drop current meter (grounded).   **Figure 8.12.** Same floating.

lowing to ground (or to points of zero potential). Battery operation removes this restriction. The circuit of Figure 8.12 is as flexible as the meter itself; it can be used to measure current flow between points that are thousands of volts above ground.

The circuit above does not lend itself to the measurement of currents greater than the range of the meter movement; it is limited in any event to currents within the output current rating of the amplifier—usually 2 milliamperes. However, scaling for currents *smaller* than the meter range is easy enough, and this is where practical need usually lies. Figure 8.13 shows how it is done. A current divider comprising R_1 and R_2 dictates that the amplifier output must deliver—through the meter—not only the measured current but also an additional current related to it by the ratio of the resistors, as stated by the formula in the figure. A concrete example to follow is predicated upon the use of an operational amplifier of the field-effect transistor or F.E.T. input type. The reason

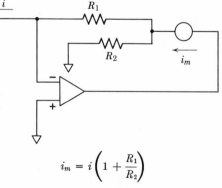

$$i_m = i\left(1 + \frac{R_1}{R_2}\right)$$

Figure 8.13. Current-multiplying zero-drop meter.

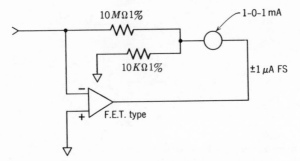

Figure 8.14.   One-microampere full-scale instrument.

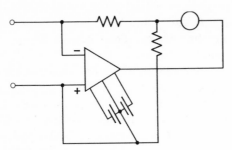

Figure 8.15.   Same floating.

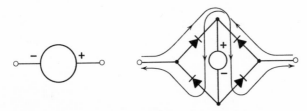

Figure 8.16.   Comparison of dc and ac current meters.

for this stipulation will become clear in the chapter on amplifier errors
along with a method of using an ordinary amplifier to achieve the result.
Figure 8.14 is the schematic of a zero-drop instrument reading ±1-micro-
ampere full scale. It resolves 10 nanoamperes (10×10^{-9}) and with a
1%-meter movement the accuracy is on the same order. If battery
powered in the manner shown in Figure 8.15, the whole instrument fits
in the palm of the hand—or even inside the meter case. This performance
carries only one proviso: this circuit is not adapted to measuring currents

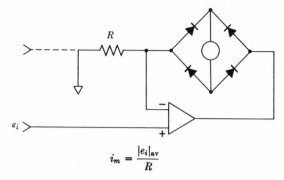

$$i_m = \frac{|e_i|_{av}}{R}$$

Figure 8.17.   High-resistance ac voltmeter.

from low-resistance sources. In particular, situations where the circuit is connected to resistances as low as 100,000 ohms are to be avoided.

The preferred circuits of this chapter place the meter in the feedback path. Substitution of an ac meter converts them into precise alternating current instruments. Figure 8.16 shows how an ac meter is constructed from a dc meter and a diode bridge. Arrows in the figure trace the paths of the rectified ac currents. The various circuits are redrawn with the diode bridge added in Figures 8.17 to 8.20. As pointed out earlier, the magnitude of meter current is set by the operational circuit; the diodes steer the current in the proper direction through the meter but are otherwise powerless to influence it. In other words, the high gain of the operational amplifier renders the diodes ideal.

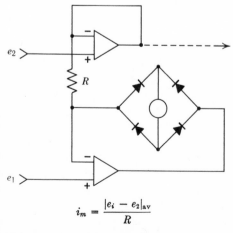

$$i_m = \frac{|e_i - e_2|_{av}}{R}$$

Figure 8.18.   High-resistance differential ac voltmeter.

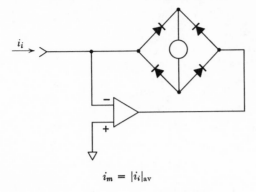

$$i_m = |i_i|_{av}$$

Figure 8.19.   Zero-drop ac current meter.

There is no explicit provision in the circuits for rejecting direct current; they respond to any dc signal present (voltage or current as the case may be). The result is that the behavior for small signals (on the same order as the dc level) is aberrated. For sinusoidal signals substantially larger than the dc level the effect averages out, but for other signals, pulselike signals in particular, external means of removing the dc must be provided (for example, a blocking capacitor).

These ac meter circuits are said to be average-reading or average-responding circuits. This means that the reading is proportional to the area between the waveform and its zero axis. Specifically, the reading is *not* simply related to the energy content of the signal, unless the waveform is known and known to be pure. It is common practice to

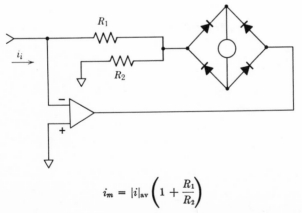

$$i_m = |i|_{av}\left(1 + \frac{R_1}{R_2}\right)$$

Figure 8.20.   Current-amplifying zero-drop ac meter.

interpret an average reading in terms of an "equivalent rms" for a given waveform, usually a sinusoid, but much more than 1% error can result from distortion, even in a signal that appears to be perfect on an oscilloscope. True root-mean-square computer circuit modules are available from the manufacturers of operational amplifiers.

Differential measurements can be made with the circuits of Figures 8.4 and 8.17 in the case where one of the points to be measured can deliver the meter current, for example, when it is the output of an amplifier. The procedure is to lift the metering resistor from its ground connection and drive it as an input with the low-impedance input source, as suggested by the dashed lines in the figures. Particularly in the ac case the economy of this means of measurement is notable.

Chapter IX

Amplifier Errors—Input Voltage and Current

The preceding chapters have presented circuitry that is understandable and usable without knowledge of the imperfections of the operational amplifiers; indeed it was pointed out as one of the charms of the technology that much could be done while almost ignoring the amplifier itself. Naturally much more can be done given knowledge of the sources of error and techniques of compensation, when it is possible, and of evasion, when it is not.

In earlier chapters the operational circuit was taken to be in equilibrium when the voltage difference between the amplifier input terminals was zero; this assumption will now be refined. In real amplifiers an input error voltage shifts the point of equilibrium slightly away from zero volts. This voltage error is a composite of several sources, functions of time, temperature, frequency, and so on (including random processes). For the moment all of these demons may be housed conceptually in a source of voltage uncertainty placed in series with the input terminals. This error voltage source, and it *is* a voltage source akin to a battery from a circuit theory standpoint, may be placed in either input lead. Figure 9.1 demonstrates that it is immaterial in which lead the source is placed, provided that the polarity of its series connection is preserved. It is easiest to locate the error source in the direct input lead; there it appears and behaves as an input signal source (which it is, albeit an unwanted one). In Figure 9.1*a* the simple follower reproduces the input error voltage at the output, thus nulling the input difference voltage of the inner amplifier, which is presumed error-free. In Figure 9.1b the output must seek that voltage which renders the input difference zero. In more complex circuits it is almost always easier to assess the effects of input voltage error by localizing it as a source in the direct input lead.

A second assumption about the operational amplifier was that its inputs allowed zero current flow. This assumption, like the voltage assumption above, is now changed to the status of a first approximation justified by its utility, which is undiminished. Input error currents are shown as current sources in parallel with the input terminals of the heretofore

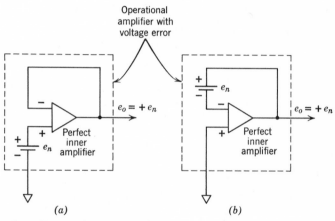

(a)   *(b)*

Figure 9.1.   Input voltage uncertainty.

perfect amplifier in Figure 9.2. The operational circuit is the current-to-voltage transducer with its signal current set identically to zero by an open circuit. The error current of the direct input has no effect because the input is grounded. The error current of the inverting input is transduced by the feedback resistor into an erroneous output voltage, in that it signifies a signal current that is not present. It is, however, an impeccable measurement of the error current, this being the circuit used for that purpose.

A sketch of the physics of these errors lends concreteness to the argument even though it applies only to amplifiers with conducting-junction transistor input stages. See Figure 9.3. The input circuit comprises a pair of transistors matched or manufactured to be as nearly alike as possible. That is, when the principal currents in the devices (the collector currents) are equal, then the input voltages (base-emitter voltage or V_{BE}) and the input currents (base current or i_B) of the pair should match. It is clear that equalities of this sort can be neither exact nor invariant with time and environmental change. An exact match of the transistor voltages implies an amplifier free of voltage error. The input currents are still a nuisance even if they match exactly, as for example, when the circuit of Figure 9.2 is used to measure an external signal current. However, given near equality of these currents and their tendency to track with temperature, even though they are strong and nonlinear functions thereof, a number of balanced-circuit schemes may be used to

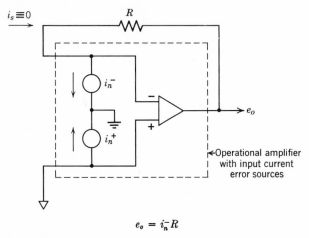

$$e_o = i_n^- R$$

Figure 9.2. Input current uncertainty.

advantage. In the final analysis it is the difference between the input currents that causes an irreducible error in the operational circuit. Other amplifier types have different physical mechanisms underlying these two fundamental errors, but may be thought about by the methods given here. The schemes of input-current compensation apply principally to transistor amplifiers, however, and to integrated-circuit types in particular.

As indicated above the error currents at both inputs are of interest as is their difference. Figure 9.4 gives the test circuit for error current at the direct input. The circuit action is not entirely obvious. In Figure 9.2 the inverting input must be at zero volts because the direct input is grounded; the output moves positive to drive the error current through the feedback resistor. Thus Ohm's law provides that the output voltage is a measure of the error current. In Figure 9.4 the amplifier is connected as a simple follower with the test resistor connecting the direct input

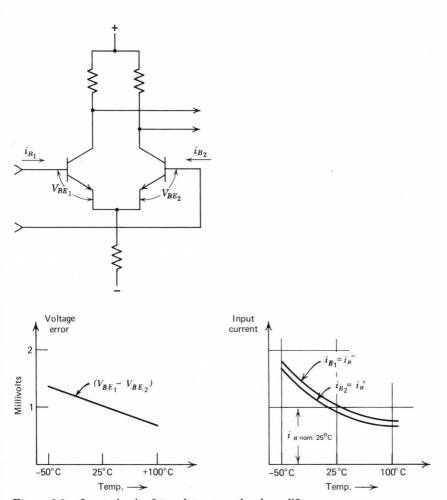

Figure 9.3.   Input circuit of transistor operational amplifier.

to ground. The voltage at all three amplifier terminals must be the same; consequently the whole circuit "droops" negative in voltage until the voltage drop across the test resistor suffices to provide the error current demanded by the direct input.

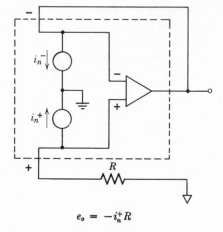

$$e_o = -i_n^+ R$$

Figure 9.4. Test circuit for current at direct input.

The difference between the input currents is measured by superposition of the two circuits as shown in Figure 9.5. Although a more direct application of the notion of superposition is not easy to find, the circuit action may not be entirely clear. In any event an explanation is justified by the importance of this kind of technique in operational circuitry. The voltage at the direct input is set by its own error current flowing

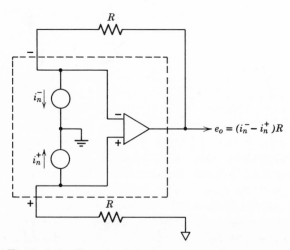

Figure 9.5. Test circuit for input current-tracking error.

through the test resistor, causing the terminal to droop below ground potential as described above. If the error current at the inverting input were zero, the voltage of the direct input would appear by follower action at the output, where, by the same assumption, it would be a true measure of error current difference. Voltage drop across the feedback resistor, which is caused by and is a measure of the error current at the inverting input, is added algebraically to the voltage at the direct input because the voltage difference between the inputs must be zero. Thus the output voltage equals the algebraic sum of the drop in the direct input resistor and the rise across the feedback resistor, a sum

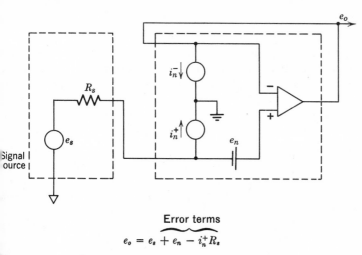

Error terms
$$e_o = e_s + e_n - i_n^+ R_s$$

Figure 9.6.   Voltage and current errors in simple follower.

which may be seen to be zero when the input currents match. The test resistors must be large so that amplifier voltage errors can be neglected.

The voltage follower is a high-resistance voltage-readout circuit; ideally it does not draw current from the signal source. It is shown together with amplifier error sources in Figure 9.6. Amplifier voltage error is a direct measurement error about which nothing can be done except to use an amplifier having better specifications. Input current causes error by inducing it in the resistance of the signal source. This error is usually dominant with amplifiers using ordinary transistors. By way of illustration the errors caused by temperature variation are given for a typical microcircuit amplifier. It is conventional to quote a temperature coefficient specifying the rate of change of the parameter with temperature:

$$\text{voltage error: 10 microvolts/°C } (10^{-5} \text{ volt/°C}) = \frac{\partial v}{\partial \theta}$$

$$\text{current error: 3 nanoamperes/°C } (3 \times 10^{-9} \text{ ampere/°C}) = \frac{\partial i}{\partial \theta}$$

$$\theta = \text{temperature}$$

The signal source resistance, R_s, for which the current error equals the voltage error is found by dividing the coefficients. It follows that for source resistances exceeding 3333 ohms the current error dominates, even though the input *resistance* of the follower, as discussed in Chapter 4, exceeds 200 megohms. Another comparison is that to make a current equal to the error current at room temperature flow into the 200-megohm input resistance, a voltage of some 60 volts is required. Since 10 millivolts (0.01 volt) is an ordinary maximum signal level for this circuit when used as a preamplifier, the magnitude of the input current error can be appreciated. It is a problem not only in the voltage follower but in almost all circuits except those serving high-level, very low-resistance signal sources (such as the outputs of preceding operational circuits).

In the follower case an improvement by about a factor of 10 can be had for the price of one resistor, provided that the source resistance is known and constant to within 1 part in 10. The current-compensated follower is shown in Figure 9.7; it will be recognized as the configuration of Figure 9.5. A small capacitor is shown across the compensating resistor for dynamic stability, as explained in the next chapter. In addition to the temperature compensation achieved because the input currents track closely with temperature, there is also cancellation of the gross input error due to current at any given temperature by about the same factor. Seldom does one resistor serve so well.

This artifice can be applied to followers with current meters in the feedback like those of Chapter 8. See Figure 9.8. Here the operational circuit behaves as if the direct output were at point A and the inverting input were at point B. The actual input terminals droop in voltage due to the input currents flowing in the resistors R_s, but the only effect of this is that the inputs operate at a slightly more negative common-mode voltage. The amplifier error current flows in the meter unamplified and is negligible.

Note well that these techniques do not prevent the input current from flowing in the signal source and are of no avail when the current itself is objectionable (as perhaps in certain biological measurements) or when the nature of the source will not allow a dc current (for example, a

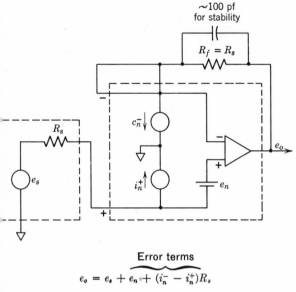

Error terms

$$e_o = e_s + \overbrace{e_n + (i_n^- - i_n^+)R_s}$$

Figure 9.7. Current-compensated voltage follower.

capacitive transducer). Remedies for these cases will be forthcoming, notably in the chapter on instrumentation.

The current follower or current-to-voltage transducer circuit is the second most basic circuit after the voltage follower, and since it uses the same configuration just exploited to achieve current compensation, it is reasonable to examine it with the same end in view. The circuit

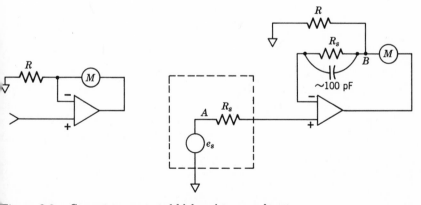

Figure 9.8. Current-compensated high-resistance voltmeter.

is drawn in Figure 9.9 together with a different kind of signal source. A current source has its associated resistance placed in parallel, contrasting with the series connection of the source resistance of a voltage source. An ideal or pure current source is drawn without the resistor as is a pure voltage source, but the implication is opposite in each case. A perfect current source has the resistance of an open circuit, whereas a perfect voltage source has that of a short circuit.

It is clear from Figure 9.9 that the error current of the inverting input causes a direct error by draining some of the signal current that

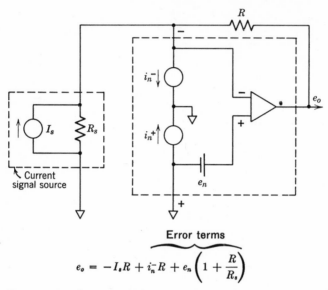

$$e_o = -I_s R + i_n^- R + e_n \left(1 + \frac{R}{R_s}\right)$$

Figure 9.9.   Current-to-voltage transducer with current and voltage error sources.

would be transduced into output voltage by the feedback resistor. It is necessary to devise some means of substituting the much smaller difference of the error currents for the gross error current; as things stand the potentially compensatory error current of the direct input flows from ground without good or ill effect. The compensation scheme is shown in Figure 9.10. It lets the input terminals droop below ground potential and balances the input currents against each other so that only their difference causes error at the output. The signal current is superposed with the error current in the feedback resistor and transduced into output voltage just as if it were the only current component (thanks to the resistor as a linear element). There is a catch, however, when the signal source resistance is relatively small. The voltage droop induces an error current to flow in the source resistance R_s. If $R_s = R$, the metering resistor, nothing has been gained, but if it is several times larger, the trick is worth doing. If the source is essentially a perfect current source the trick is done: error current difference has been substituted for gross error current.

Knowledge of the value of the source resistance enables current compensation without the restriction above. The resistor in the direct input

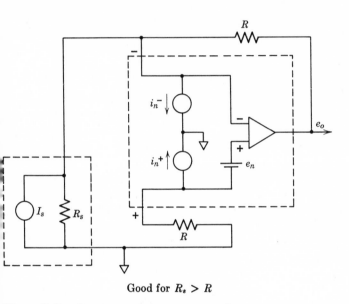

Good for $R_s > R$

Figure 9.10.   Input-error current compensation.

is made equal to the parallel combination of the source resistance and the feedback resistor. The scheme is shown in Figure 9.11 along with the relevant algebra, for those who enjoy the clank of factors dropping out of equations. Note that the effect of voltage error rises for small values of source resistance, compensation or not. For source resistances low enough to cause trouble there is some question as to the wisdom of making a high-quality current measurement of this type.

Current compensation is inherent in a differential measurement of the current from two sources or from a single floating source (see Figure 9.12). Two very similar amplifiers are required and they must be closely

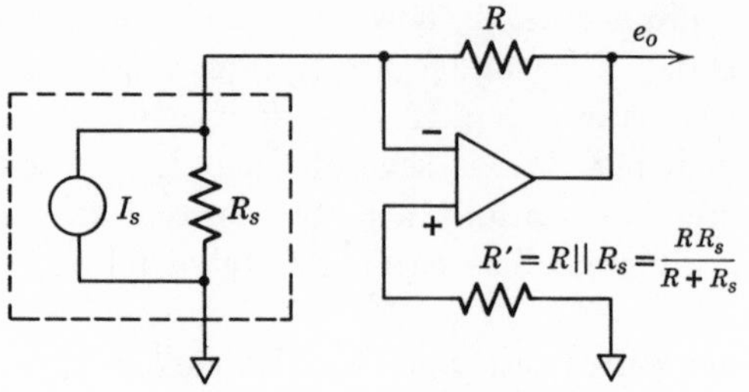

$$R' = R \| R_s = \frac{R R_s}{R + R_s}$$

$$e_o = -i_s R - i_n^+ \left(\frac{R R_s}{R + R_s} \right) \left(\frac{R_s + R}{R_s} \right) + i_n^- R$$
$$+ e_n \left(1 + \frac{R}{R_s} \right)$$

Figure 9.11. Input current compensation for known source resistance.

coupled thermally. This means that two microcircuit amplifiers in a single package are implied for a thoroughly practical embodiment, although the scheme does have some other utility in a laboratory context. The lower amplifier in each case supplies the error current for itself and for the output amplifier, as indicated by the arrows in the figure. If the voltage errors in the amplifiers track with temperature, as is the case with microcircuit amplifiers, then errors from this source will be self-compensating to some degree. When a true zero-drop and zero-volt current determination is to be made, Figure 9.12a is the circuit

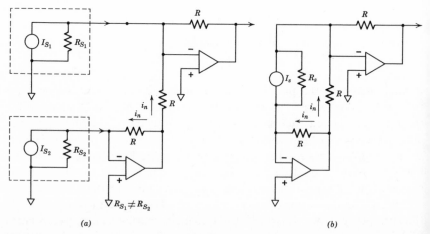

(a)   (b)

Figure 9.12. Inherent current compensation.

of choice. If a single source is to be measured the bottom amplifier is open-circuited, which is to say, it is connected to a pure current source of zero current.

Circuits possessing symmetry are inherently compensated for input current error; the structures of Chapter 5 are exemplary. Even nonlinear

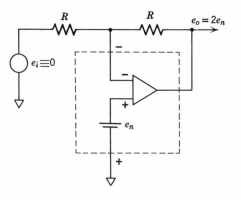

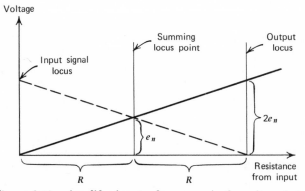

Figure 9.13. Amplifier input-voltage error in the unity-gain inverter.

circuits can sometimes be balanced; an absolute value circuit having this property appears in the computation chapter.

The unity-gain invertor circuit has the rather surprising property of being twice as susceptible as the simple follower to amplifier voltage error. This is easily shown in a voltage-resistance graph (see Figure 9.13). Setting the input signal to zero, which is synonymous with *grounding* the operational circuit input, and placing the error voltage source in the direct input, the follower-with-gain of two configuration obtains with respect to the error voltage. The diagram is drawn by plotting the error voltage on the summing point locus (because the input terminals of the inner error-free amplifier must stay together in voltage), and then drawing the line of constant current through the zero input signal point. What of the effect of input current error on the "constant" current line? The answer is that the line acquires a bend at the summing point locus as will be pointed out presently; the procedure is to treat the two kinds of error separately and superpose. The dashed line on the diagram shows that an input signal twice as large as the error voltage is required to bring the output voltage to zero, the error masquerading as a signal twice its size. What is happening is that the output signal is attenuated by the resistor network in the process of being fed back to the inverting input, and attenuation in the feedback path causes magnification in the forward path. This phenomenon is called *noise gain* and is a perennial concern. Interestingly enough its origin is in no way electronic; it arises from the problem in metrology of comparing quantities of different size.

The next topic sounds prosaic enough: input current errors in the unity-gain invertor. Its importance resides in the close relation of the invertor to the integrator, perhaps the most important circuit and one which is utterly at the mercy of current errors. The invertor circuit with current error sources is shown in Figure 9.14 along with the correct but far from obvious V-R plot. Having plotted both the input signal and the summing point at zero volts, one can draw the horizontal line between them and conclude that the current in the input resistor must be zero. This is correct but not very helpful. From where does the error current come? The only possibility is through the feedback resistor. The output voltage moves up to drive the error current through the resistor to the inverting input. The circuit behaves exactly like the test circuit of Figure 9.12. Again, this is not obvious; all that can be said is that knowing that the invertor behaves in this way makes it easier to guess the behavior of more complex circuits. The V-R diagram summarizes the result, even though it was of little help in deducing it. A slope discontinuity occurs at the summing point locus; the change in slope is equal to the input error current.

The size of the error thus incurred is sufficient even in the case of the simple invertor to motivate efforts at current compensation. The error in volts is the product of the input current and the feedback resistance. It amounts to some 3 millivolts for a $10K$-$10K$ invertor made with a typical transistor amplifier; not much but enough to violate an accuracy specification of 0.01% in a 10-volt full-scale system. Current compensation is achieved by placing in series with the direct input a resistance equal to the parallel combination of all resistors connected to the inverting input—$5K$ is correct in this example. The compensated invertor appears in Figure 9.15. The V-R plot is more helpful here, especially if one observes that current in the diagram flows "downhill," that is, from higher to lower potential. The compensating resistor causes

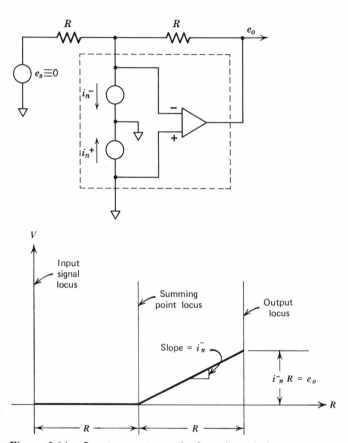

Figure 9.14. Input current error in the unity-gain inverter.

the inputs to operate below ground by half of the original output error voltage. The result is that the input and feedback resistors share the error current equally, and the error voltage at the output is zero. Or, more exactly, the output error would be zero if the input currents matched. Even so, the net has been substituted for the gross error current, with the attendant improvement in temperature stability. If individual trimming is practical the $5K$ resistor should be trimmed to zero the output. The equivalent resistance rule is quite general, applying to gains other than 1, to multiple-input summation circuits, and, as will be shown below, to integrators and differentiators as well.

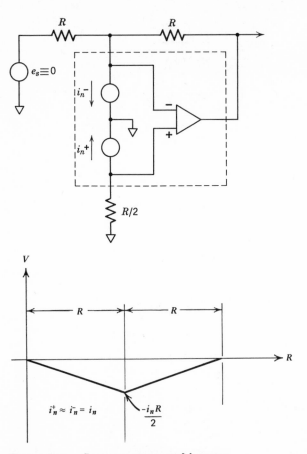

Figure 9.15.   Current-compensated invertor.

The current compensation scheme can be carried further. By making the compensating resistor equal to the input resistor, all the inverting input error current can be made to flow in the input resistor—and thus the *error current in the feedback element is zero*. Figure 9.16 illustrates the situation; the error voltage at the output is the negative of its value in the uncompensated invertor. Now if a capacitor replaces the feedback resistor, the resulting integrator will not drift.

The pace of the preceding paragraph was swift and calls for a recapitulation. The uncompensated invertor with which the discussion started is converted into an integrator in Figure 9.17 by changing the

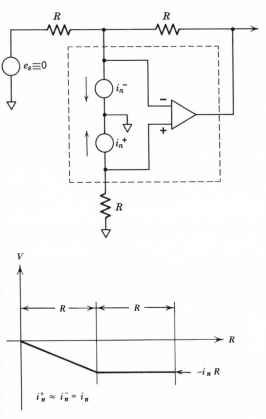

Figure 9.16.   Overcompensated invertor.

feedback element to a capacitor. It was pointed out that all the error current flowed in the feedback element. In Chapter 3 it was stated that a capacitor could deliver a direct current given a constant rate of change of voltage across it. This is exactly how the input current is provided in Figure 9.17; the output moves positively at a rate sufficient to drive the error current through the capacitor. This rate is 0.3 volt per second for an integrator made with 1 microfarad and a typical transistor operational amplifier—clearly the circuit is useless in this form except perhaps for a certain very high-speed, short computing-epoch service. The usual practice is to provide a fixed bias current equal to the gross input current at some temperature in the range of service temperature expected, here

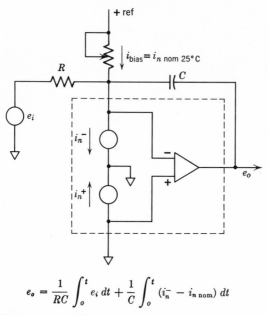

$$e_o = \frac{1}{RC} \int_0^t e_i \, dt + \frac{1}{C} \int_0^t (i_n^- - i_{n\,\text{nom}}) \, dt$$

Figure 9.17.   Uncompensated integrator.

taken as 25° centigrade for simplicity. Thus a current equal to what has been called $i_{n\,\text{nom}\,25°C}$ in Figure 9.3 is supplied through a high-value bias resistor from the positive reference voltage. This expedient does not take account of the variation of the error current with temperature; that is, it is correct for only one point on the curvilinear function given in Figure 9.3. The integrator above, biased in this fashion, will drift about 3 millivolts per second for each degree of temperature excursion from the trimming temperature.

In contrast, the compensated integrator in Figure 9.18 drifts at a rate proportional to the much smaller input current difference, on the order of 30 millivolts per second without trimming, and can be easily trimmed to drift less than 1 millivolt per second with the same capacitor used above. The drift rate at temperatures other than the trimming

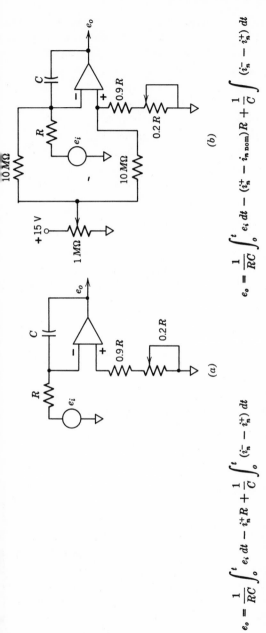

$$e_o = \frac{1}{RC} \int_o^t e_i\, dt - i_n^+ R + \frac{1}{C} \int_o^t (i_n^- - i_n^+)\, dt$$

(a)

$$e_o = \frac{1}{RC} \int_o^t e_i\, dt - (i_n^+ - i_{n\,\mathrm{nom}}) R + \frac{1}{C} \int (i_n^- - i_n^+)\, dt$$

(b)

Figure 9.18. Current-compensated integrator.

temperature is governed by the tracking of the input currents, which means for microcircuit amplifiers that it is some ten times better than the uncompensated case. An offset voltage (fixed, not a drift *rate*) equal to the drop across the compensating resistor is incurred; it can be cancelled at a given temperature by the scheme shown in *b*, but remains a function of the gross input current and thus of temperature. It is a small enough price to pay in the majority of applications.

The importance of this compensation technique derives from the soundness of compensating an input device by using its mate, which is as nearly identical as the technology allows, and which operates in the same electrical environment (supply voltage, common-mode voltage)

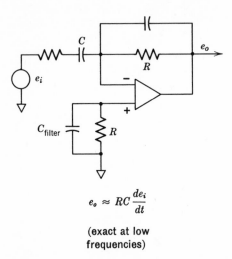

$$e_o \approx RC \frac{de_i}{dt}$$

(exact at low
frequencies)

Figure 9.19. Current-compensated differentiator.

and the same physical environment (temperature, pressure, electric and magnetic fields, et cetera). It is difficult to imagine a riper opportunity than two microtransistors made side by side on a monolithic chip. Only slightly less promising are two electrically isolated amplifiers on a single chip; indeed the additional flexibility of two amplifiers can be exploited to achieve both voltage and current compensation—sometimes simultaneously as in the differential current follower of Figure 9.12.

The differentiator circuit is well suited to error current compensation; its use entails no additional error term. A circuit for a practical differentiator appears in Figure 9.19. The added resistor and capacitor modify the response at frequencies above the highest data frequency of interest.

This is necessary both for dynamic stability and to curtail the response to the ever-present noise that a true differentiator would accentuate. The resistor in the input is ignored when applying the equivalent resistance rule because it is blocked against dc current by the capacitor. The capacitor shown in parallel with the compensating resistor serves to short out the ac components of amplifier current noise and the thermal noise generated in the usually very large, and therefore noisy, resistor. This capacitor is recommended always, having been omitted until now for simplicity. Its value is not critical, something in the range of 0.1 microfarad, but it should be of high-leakage resistance so as not to spoil the current compensation.*

Voltage and current error will now be superposed for the case of the uncompensated invertor. In Figure 9.20 the current error is shown dashed and the voltage error dotted. The errors as drawn happen to be in opposition, and this hints at the possibility of what must straightway be branded a *vicious practice*. Amplifiers are provided either with a built-in voltage zero adjustment or a terminal to which such a control may be conveniently connected. The temptation to misuse this control to cancel a current error or some other sort of output offset must be resisted. The voltage error is to be zeroed by using a circuit like that seen in Figure 9.21; after a few minutes or more of warmup the adjustment should be made and thereafter not touched. Much more than intellectual tidiness prompts this injunction; a properly zeroed amplifier exhibits optimum drift performance. Because the two kinds of error arise from distinct physical phenomena in all amplifier types, the attempt to null one against the other is quixotic. It is far better to trim up each independently, using a clear knowledge of its effects. Furthermore, when this is done a change in the operational circuit cannot have unexpected side effects, as can happen when a large uncompensated and even unsuspected error quantity is present. An example is the variable-gain summation circuit of Figure 2.5, wherein the signal gain is controlled by a variable resistor in the feedback path. It is now clear that input error current flowing in this resistor can cause significant zero shift along with the desired change in gain. The control also modulates the effect of voltage error on the output, as explained under noise gain immediately below. In short, the example should banish any thought of casual or *ad hoc* error cancellation. The question of how to arrange the obviously useful circuit of Figure 2.5 to obviate these effects will be taken up before the end of this chapter.

* See Philbrick/Nexus *Applications Manual for Operational Amplifiers* pp. 48, 49, 90 for a comprehensive treatment of the design of practical differentiators.

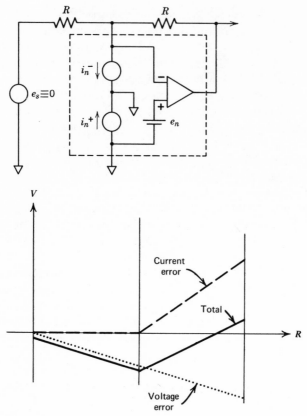

Figure 9.20. Total amplifier error.

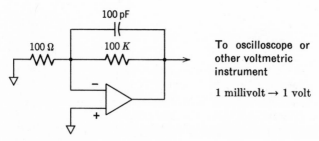

To oscilloscope or other voltmetric instrument

1 millivolt → 1 volt

Figure 9.21. Circuit for adjustment of amplifier voltage zero.

96

The term noise gain was introduced in connection with the relative disadvantage of the invertor versus the follower where voltage error is concerned; it was pointed out that error magnification was the consequence of attenuation in the feedback path. The same effect is introduced purposely in Figure 9.21 to cause the amplifier to magnify its own error voltage so that it can be measured and zeroed with a relatively crude instrument. Note, however, that if a signal source were connected to the 100-ohm resistor the signal gain would be -1000; thus in this instance the noise gain of 1001 is not a problem. Inverting circuits always have a noise gain at least greater by 1 than their signal gain, for an excellent reason set forth in the next chapter. It is when the noise gain is disproportionate to the signal gain that the problem exists. It takes several forms and is in fact a central problem facing the user-designer and the innovator of operational circuits. This topic recurs in the discussion of almost all the circuits to follow.

Some circuit features may be deceptively innocent-looking, yet warrant both study and studied avoidance. Current paths from the summing point to ground raise the noise gain; a resistive example will be given here; capacitance can be spectacularly deleterious, but that is deferred to the next chapter. At first glance it would seem that the resistor r in Figure 9.22 is harmless since it is connected between virtual ground

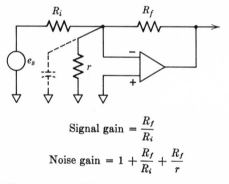

$$\text{Signal gain} = \frac{R_f}{R_i}$$

$$\text{Noise gain} = 1 + \frac{R_f}{R_i} + \frac{R_f}{r}$$

Figure 9.22. Noise-gain.

and actual ground and therefore the current in it must be zero, and for signals this reasoning is correct. As noted earlier, however, voltage error or noise behaves like a signal at the direct input. The extraneous resistor acts in parallel with the input resistor to increase the attenuation between the output and the inverting input and thus to increase the noise gain. The algebra works out so that another term is added to the expression for noise gain, which is given in the figure. If the resistor r is relatively small there is trouble; the whole spectrum of ills that have been collectively called voltage uncertainty appears at the output magnified by the noise gain. The reader might well ask: why short out the summing point with a small resistor to ground? Why indeed—it has been done though, and by some pretty smart people.

The adjustable-gain amplifier problem provides a chilling example of the pathology that sometimes entraps even the experienced clinician. It is shown in its essentials in Figure 9.23; the input error current flows

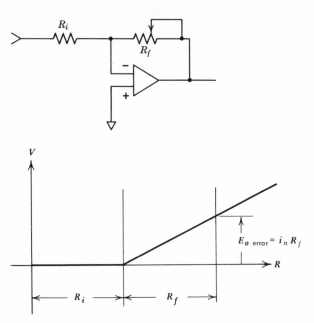

Figure 9.23.   Error-current offset in adjustable gain amplifier circuit.

in the feedback resistor and causes an output voltage offset proportional to its resistance. Figure 9.24 shows an attempted fix based on the idea of keeping the feedback resistance approximately constant. A relatively low-resistance potentiometer serves as a voltage divider to control the fraction of the output voltage connected to the feedback resistor and thus varies the effective size of the resistor. If α is the divider ratio, then the signal gain is inversely proportional to α, and the hope is that the feedback resistance is relatively unchanging with α because the

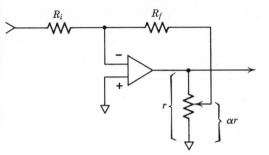

Figure 9.24. An attempted fix.

potentiometer resistance r is much smaller than R_f. Three things are wrong. First, the linear gain adjustment that was a feature of the original has been lost; instead the gain is proportional to the reciprocal of the setting α. Second, the voltage noise gain has been nearly doubled. A comparison of the noise gain of the two circuits, set up for signal gains adjustable from 1 to 10, is shown in Figure 9.25. The explanation is that the output is operated on by *two* voltage dividers in cascade in the process of getting back to the inverting input. But the most humiliating problem is that the output offset caused by current error has been

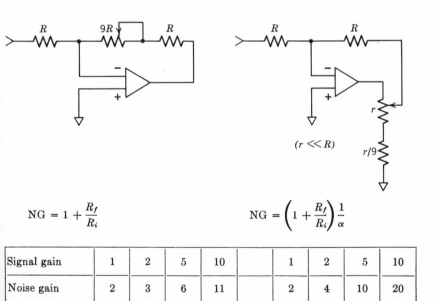

$$NG = 1 + \frac{R_f}{R_i}$$

$$NG = \left(1 + \frac{R_f}{R_i}\right)\frac{1}{\alpha}$$

Signal gain	1	2	5	10		1	2	5	10
Noise gain	2	3	6	11		2	4	10	20

Figure 9.25. Noise-gain comparison.

affected not at all. The reason is that to drive the inexorable input current through the feedback resistor the output voltage must deflect an amount inversely proportional to the potentiometer setting α. In other words, it is all too true that the effective resistance of the feedback element is controlled by the potentiometer; the effect applies to the error current exactly as it does to the signal current. The aspirant innovator is constantly exposed to hoaxes of his own devising, although this example is surely among the more outrageous. But note well, in the circuit field in particular, today's blooper properly understood is frequently the basis of tomorrow's gem.

An exact solution is current compensation using a dual potentiometer to alter the compensation resistance along with the feedback resistance. See Figure 9.26, in which the dashed lines indicate that the controls

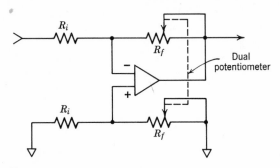

Figure 9.26. Exact current compensation.

are mechanically ganged together. Apart from the stigma of brute force the only objection is the practical one that dual potentiometers are expensive and not always available. Furthermore, they may not be obtainable at all in the multiturn types likely to be used for a calibrated circuit of this sort. Although high accuracy is clearly not needed in the compensating element, it must still be coupled somehow to the accurate feedback element. This suggests that this approach is more suitable when switched precision resistors are used as the gain-setting technique, since selector switches with several decks are cheap and commonly on hand.

A more appealing, though approximate, alternative makes use of the artifice of current overcompensation to make the error current in the feedback element zero. In Figure 9.27 the compensation resistor is made equal to the input resistor (or to the parallel combination of input resistors). Thus only the net error current flows in the feedback resistor

o cause zero shift when the resistor is varied. Secondly, the error due
o gross input current is now proportional to the input resistor, which
means that it has the same magnitude as in the original circuit at unity
gain (the sign of the error being reversed). Finally, if there are multiple
inputs the situation improves directly with their number because the
resistance through which the error current flows is correspondingly reduced. These remarks apply only to current-caused errors; the noise

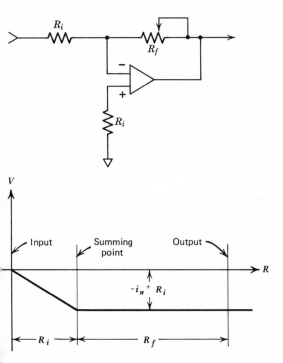

Figure 9.27a.   Overcompensation makes error current in feedback element zero.

gain for voltage error grows with the number of inputs. In summary,
for a single input near unity gain the only improvement is that the
feedback resistor does not modulate the gross error current (which was
the original complaint); for multiple inputs and gains greater than unity
the overcompensation scheme has additional advantages. For substantial
gains its performance approaches that of the exactly compensated case.
Once again, when an error component is reduced by compensation of
this sort, its temperature dependence is similarly reduced.

Returning briefly to the question of noise gain in multiple input cir cuits: noise gain or as it is called in the next chapter, feedback attenua tion factor, places a limit on the number of inputs especially at low signal levels. If low-level signals are to be summed with maximum ac curacy there is no alternative to separate preamplifiers for each signa

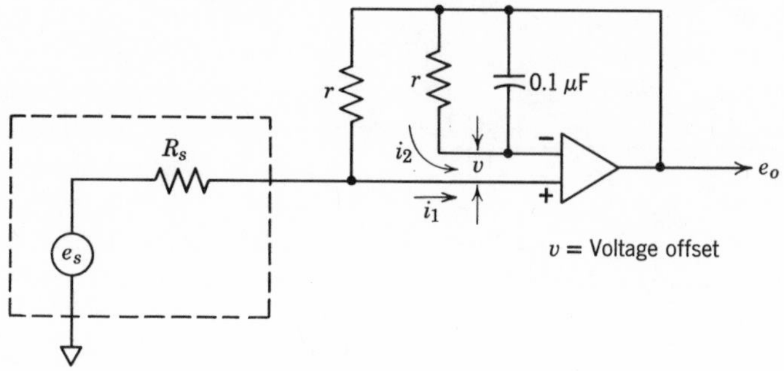

$$e_{\text{error current}} = -i_n^+ R_i + (i_n^- - i_n^+)R_f$$

$$e_o = e_s + R_s(i_2 - i_1) + i_2 r + v\left(1 + \frac{R_s}{r}\right)$$

$$\theta = \text{temperature}$$

$$\frac{\partial e_o}{\partial \theta} = \frac{\partial i_2}{\partial \theta}(R_s + r) + \frac{\partial i_1}{\partial \theta}R_s + \frac{\partial v}{\partial \theta}\left(1 + \frac{R_s}{r}\right)$$

$$\frac{d}{dr}\left(\frac{\partial e_o}{\partial \theta}\right) = \frac{\partial i_2}{\partial \theta} - \frac{\partial v}{\partial \theta}\frac{R_s}{r^2}$$

$$0 = \frac{\partial i_2}{\partial \theta} - \frac{\partial v}{\partial \theta}\frac{R_s}{r^2}$$

$$r_{\text{optimum}} = \sqrt{R_s\left(\frac{\frac{\partial v}{\partial \theta}}{\frac{\partial i_2}{\partial \theta}}\right)}$$

Figure 9.27b. A current-compensation arrangement.

using the follower-with-gain for voltage signals and the current followe for current source inputs. It is standard practice thus to get signal "up out of the mud" before attempting to process or compute with then in any way.

It is appropriate to treat voltage and current errors as static phe nomena because both have steady components that are crucial to de and low-frequency circuits, but it should be kept in mind that botl exist over the entire frequency spectrum. Fortunately there is a strong analogy in the way steady errors and noise of whatever elevated frequency are handled—both conceptually and practically. Unfortunately the current compensation schemes presented at such length here have no relevance to other than steady errors, since ac noise at the two inputs is not correlated. A treatment of noise will not be attempted. It should be remarked in passing that the noise performance of operational amplifiers has prompted the beginnings of a literature on their use in low-noise preamplifiers, a rather specialized field of engineering endeavor.

Since this chapter was written a development in connection with the instrumentation amplifiers of Chapter 11 appears relevant to simple followers as well. The configuration and the results of a short analysis are given in Figure 9.27b. This scheme is a means of trading voltage drift for current drift; it allows transistor amplifiers to be used with what would otherwise be prohibitively high source resistances. When the scheme is used with simple followers there is a substantial voltage offset that is canceled in the differential circuits for which it was conceived. Nevertheless, it is attractive for simple followers when the source resistance is high and variable or unknown. Note that even for low-resistance sources the performance does not utterly deteriorate—it is just that the offset is larger than would be the case if the compensation resistors were omitted.

The scheme substitutes net input current for gross input current without requiring accurate knowledge of the source resistance. The quotient of partial derivatives in the expression for $r_{optimum}$ may be taken as the characteristic noise resistance of the operational amplifier. The expression then says that the compensation resistors should be made equal to the geometric mean of the source resistance and the amplifier characteristic resistance. Typically an improvement approaching a factor of 10 is achieved in overall temperature drift with a 10-megohm source and a transistor microcircuit amplifier with $100K$ compensation resistors. Note that a capacitor is indicated across the feedback compensation resistor.

Chapter X

Dynamic Error and Stability

The other major class of error in operational circuitry is dynamical, although a purely static case is subsumed here for reasons of context.

In Chapter 1 the operational amplifier was characterized as a time integrator cascaded with a substantial voltage amplification. Figure 10.1 gives the actual gain versus frequency response of general-purpose operational amplifiers. Except at very low frequencies, the integrator characterization is correct, and it will be shown that the consequences of the low-frequency discrepancy are circumscribed and easily predicted. The response is shown on linear scales at the left of the figure to call attention to the hyperbolic character of the function: the gain is the reciprocal of the frequency. The more usual (and useful) presentation is on the logarithmic scales at the right. The extremely high gain of the integrator at very low frequencies is not duplicated by the amplifier; instead a constant gain called the dc voltage gain, A_{dc}, is provided.

The explanations of Chapter 1 used a dc signal and an amplifier with the gain properties of a true time integrator; thus, like those control systems having an integrator in the control loop, the error at equilibrium was zero. This expository convenience can now be abandoned and the effect of finite amplifier gain placed in evidence. Finite gain implies that the summing-point voltage is not zero at equilibrium; in particular, there is a proportionality between the output voltage and input difference voltage, the constant of proportionality being the gain by definition.

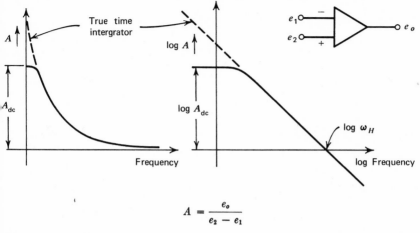

$$A = \frac{e_o}{e_2 - e_1}$$

Figure 10.1. Gain versus frequency for the operational amplifier. (Sinusoidal input signals.)

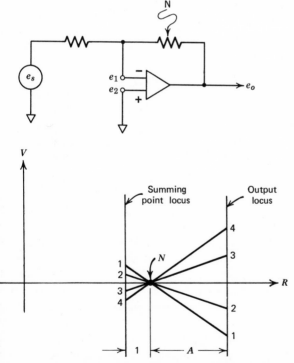

Figure 10.2. Graphical interpretation of amplifier open-loop gain.

This observation is expressed graphically in Figure 10.2; for every output voltage the corresponding summing point voltage is mapped by a ray passing through the point labeled N in the diagram. If the gain is A, point N must be located as shown between the loci of the summing point and the output. Point N is a voltage null, having an actual physical location near the summing-point end of the feedback resistor. The existence of this point makes possible the graphical and analytical solutions given in Figure 10.3 for an inverting amplifier of finite gain but otherwise free of imperfection. The dashed line is the correct equilibrium state approached when the gain is very large. Evidently an error in the magnification factor relating input signal and output voltage is the only effect of the finite gain. It would seem that this error could be "calibrated out" by altering the resistor ratio appropriately, and it could, except that this vitiates the whole idea of a feedback technology. Instead the gain is made sufficiently large so that the error becomes acceptably small. Observe that the circuit behaves as if a gain-related fraction of the feedback resistor had become a part of the input resistor; the analytical expression clearly embodies this viewpoint. For smaller input resistors, that is, for higher signal gains, the error incurred is seen to be more serious. Other means are available for calculating error and are superior to the phenomenological one given here, especially for circuits with multiple inputs.

The forgoing is thought to be exhaustive of the dc and very low frequency case in which the dc voltage gain of the amplifier is operative. However, it is not restricted to low frequencies. At any frequency the open-loop gain of the amplifier may be read from a graph like that of Figure 10.1 and used to predict the response of the circuit for a sinusoidal signal. As shown below, however, very fluent methods exist that use the frequency response graph itself as a design basis.

Figure 10.4 is an exercise in parallelism: the transfer operator A in the forward path of the block diagram is identically the voltage open-loop gain of the operational amplifier; the feedback transfer operator β corresponds with the attenuation factor of the feedback network [to be concrete $\beta = R_i/(R_f + R_i)$]; the algebraic summation represents the voltage subtraction at the differential inputs of the amplifier. The block diagram is the now classical representation of a feedback control system. Its overall transfer function and error transfer function are derived in Figure 10.5; the simple algebra is worth following even for that estimable reader to whom all analytical mathematics is the work of Satan. The resulting approximate equalities are the fundamental theorem of feedback technique and technology. The algebra asserts that the gain of the follower-with-gain is the reciprocal of the feedback factor,

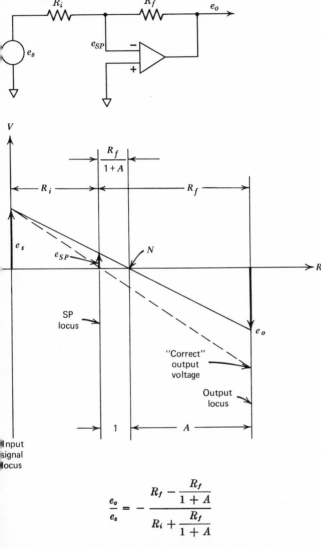

$$\frac{e_o}{e_s} = -\;\frac{R_f - \dfrac{R_f}{1+A}}{R_i + \dfrac{R_f}{1+A}}$$

Figure 10.3. Inverting amplifier circuit with finite gain A.

which agrees with the observation in Chapter 4 that the amplifier circuit undoes what the voltage divider does. A new and important fact emerges from the expression for fractional error: the product of the amplifier open-loop gain and the feedback factor β is what determines the error. This product is called the *loop gain* or the gain in the loop. It is calculated by breaking the loop at any point and proceeding around it com-

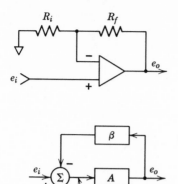

Figure 10.4. A familiar circuit and its feedback-theory representation.

pletely, multiplying together all the gains and attenuation factors. In the follower-with-gain case it is especially easy to determine the loop gain by inspection if the loop is broken between inverting input and the feedback network, because the amplifier inverting input presents the same high impedance to the network as the direct input does to the signal source—and for exactly the same reasons.

This last point is worthy of elaboration; it is important, subtle, the basis of an important circuit, and has not been made in public print. Figure 10.6 states the case; bootstrapping is the principle; it is more difficult to see with the source floating in the inverting input lead because of the inversion, but in both cases the closed loop reacts so as to minimize

Input-output transfer function:

$$e_o = A(e_i - \beta e_o)$$
$$e_o(1 + A\beta) = Ae_i$$

$$\boxed{\frac{e_o}{e_i} = \frac{A}{1 + A\beta} \approx \frac{1}{\beta} \quad \text{if} \quad A \gg 1}$$

Error transfer function:

$$\text{Fractional error} = \frac{e_i - \beta e_o}{e_i}$$

$$= \frac{e_i - \beta e_i\left(\dfrac{A}{1 + A\beta}\right)}{e_i}$$

$$= \frac{1 + A\beta - A\beta}{1 + A\beta}$$

$$\boxed{\begin{array}{l}\text{Fractional} \\ \text{error}\end{array} = \frac{1}{1 + A\beta} \approx \frac{1}{A\beta} \approx 0 \\ \qquad\qquad\qquad \text{if} \quad A\beta \gg 1}$$

Figure 10.5. The Devil's work.

the flow of current from the signal source. The application is to high-resistance voltage readout (voltage-follower service), with a single-ended amplifier such as a chopper-stabilized type. It can be done in this way when the source can float or is naturally floating. Finally, what is true of the source must be true of the feedback network in series with it. As stated, the action here is subtle, but it should not elude a reader who has persisted to this point. Note that the expression in parenthesis in the equation is the loop gain.

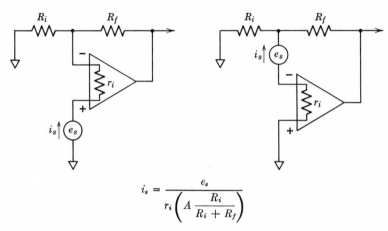

$$i_s = \frac{e_s}{r_i \left(A \dfrac{R_i}{R_i + R_f} \right)}$$

Figure 10.6.   Two equivalent cases of bootstrapping.

It is now appropriate to deal briefly with two-element RC networks, simple but seminal circuits doomed by their simplicity to be taught long before they can be appreciated in a context of high and vital technology. A first-order lag network is shown in Figure 10.7; it is so called because the output voltage for a sinusoidal input has a lagging phase angle at all frequencies, except those very much lower than the characteristic frequency, $1/RC$. The graph shows that the phase angle is 45° at the characteristic frequency and approaches 90° at high frequency. Both phase and amplitude response at high frequency are those of an integrator. The term lag is equally if less precisely descriptive of the transient response, which is seen to be a laggardly affair. A great many effects in nature and society exhibit this response, and experience with them is germane to the electrical case.

The circuit behaves as it does because the resistor limits the current flowing to charge the capacitor and therefore limits the rate of change of voltage across it. Furthermore, as charge does accumulate, the voltage difference available to drive current through the resistor is progressively reduced. Thus an equilibrium state is approached asymptotically.

A somewhat different line of physical reasoning seems suited to the step response of the lead network, Figure 10.8. Initially the charge on the capacitor is zero and it cannot change instantly; that is, a finite current must flow for a finite time to change the charge on a capacitor. Accordingly the voltage across the resistor jumps immediately to the

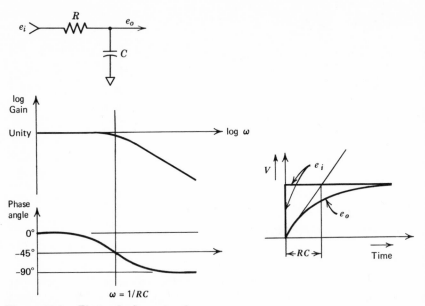

Figure 10.7.   First-order lag network.

value of the applied step and then decays as the charge on the capacitor grows. The capacitor ends fully charged to the step voltage, and the final current is zero. The resistor voltage records the current in the series circuit. It is rather startling to observe that the circuit is the *same,* the difference between lead and lag being determined by whether the output is taken across the resistor or the capacitor.

The phase of the output leads the input in the sinusoidal steady state, this somehow distressing circumstance being a manifestation of the energy storage property of the capacitor—energy from the previous cycle appearing in the present one. Examples of lead-network behavior do not abound in common experience; the lead network is an approximate differentiator just as the lag is an approximate integrator. It is also more difficult to rationalize the name *lead* in terms of the transient response; certainly the response is prompt, although actual *anticipation* of the input is a mind boggler as well as being nonsense. One ends lamely with a reference to the excellent high-frequency response.

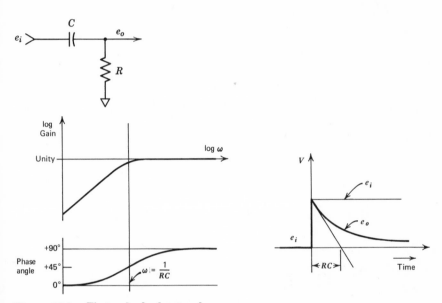

Figure 10.8.   First-order lead network.

A glance at the amplitude response in Figures 10.7 and 10.8 makes clear why the circuits are called low pass and high pass in a signal filter context.

The multiplicative property of graphical addition of functions plotted on logarithmic scales is the basis of the most widely used technique of dynamic design; it is due to Bode, and the log-log graph of open-loop response on which it is practiced is called a Bode plot. Figure 10.9 is an example of such a plot and will be used to analyze a follower-with-gain of 10. The amplifier is characterized by an integratorlike response above the very lowest frequencies; its open-loop amplitude response passes through unity gain at a frequency ω_H, which in a typical general-purpose amplifier would be 10^7 radians per second or 1.6 megahertz.

The feedback factor β is 0.1 and is independent of frequency. The reciprocal of β is also plotted. Note that the hatched area between curve A and the $1/\beta$ line represents the log of the quantity $A\beta$; that is, log $A - \log 1/\beta = \log A + \log \beta = \log A\beta$. Thus the loop gain is placed in evidence as a function of frequency merely by plotting $1/\beta$ on the frequency response graph. For frequencies for which the loop gain is

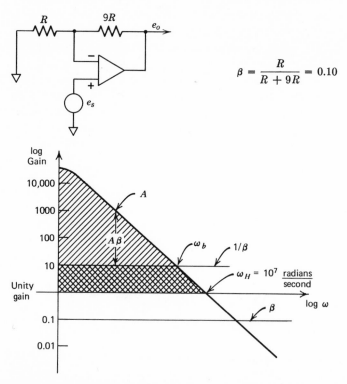

$$\beta = \frac{R}{R + 9R} = 0.10$$

Figure 10.9.   Relations among various open- and closed-loop quantities.

large, $1/\beta$ is the signal gain for the follower-with-gain, and it is an approximation to the signal gain near the point where A and $1/\beta$ intersect. Above this frequency the loop gain is fractional, and for practical purposes there is no loop, the response being that of the open-loop amplifier. The circuit behaves like a gain of 10 in cascade with a low-pass filter having a characteristic frequency equal to the intersection frequency, labeled ω_b in the figure. Thus the cross-hatched region represents an approximation to the closed-loop signal gain, which becomes exact at frequencies where the loop gain, and thus the accuracy, are high. The exact frequency response is academic because the circuit is not used at data frequencies where its own dynamic response affects the result. In the present case the characteristic frequency or *break* or *corner* frequency of the amplifier circuit occurs at 160,000 hertz, which would justify its use in the audio range below 20,000 hertz without concern for dynamic error. It is of course feasible to estimate errors of phase and amplitude by treating the amplifier as a first-order low-pass system, but the results are only estimates because the amplifier gain-crossover frequency can neither be known with precision nor assumed constant. On the contrary, the preferred approach to precision is to make both the gain and frequency response of the open-loop amplifier so high that the exact values are irrelevant. From Figure 10.5 the fractional error is understood to be the reciprocal of the loop gain $A\beta$. If the loop gain at the highest data frequency is greater than G, then the dynamic error must be less than 1 part in G parts. Analogous arguments apply to phase error.

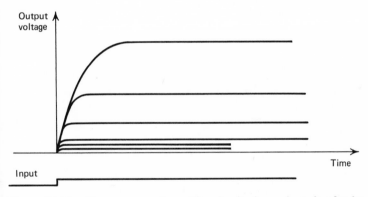

Figure 10.10.   Step response of amplifier circuits for various signal gains.

The above does not mean that dynamic response is not of interest, but only that precision is attainable only when loop gain is high. The transient response of circuits is of particular significance and may be readily predicted on the basis of the dynamic model above. The step responses of all amplifier circuits made with an amplifier of a given gain-crossover frequency are stereotypes whatever the signal gain. The greater the gain the slower the response in direct proportion. See Figure 10.10. General-purpose operational amplifiers are said to have a *constant gain-bandwidth product;* this amounts to a restatement of the earlier proposition that the open-loop gain was the reciprocal of the frequency. An amplifier arranged in this way can be operated with the widest range of feedback network configurations without becoming unstable. This open-loop characteristic yields responses for closed-loop amplifier circuits that are well-behaved, predictable, and compactly expressible.

An analysis of a follower-with-gain of generalized gain n is presented in Figure 10.11; those to whom operator calculus is a complete mystery are advised to let it remain so—on the amiable grounds that total is preferable to partial where mystery is concerned. The response is a gain of n cascaded with a first-order lag; the lag time constant is proportional to the amplification factor n and inversely proportional to the gain-crossover frequency of the amplifier, ω_H. Equivalently stated, the characteristic frequency is n times lower than ω_H. This characteristic frequency is considered to be the bandwidth of the circuit in certain fields. At this frequency the amplitude is $1/\sqrt{2}$ of its low-frequency value; it is said by some to be "3 db down," a questionable legacy from the field of psychoacoustics that has plagued electrical engineering for decades. At this frequency the loop gain falls to unity, which explains why the loop is not effective. The response to a unit step input is plotted in normalized form (simply divided by the gain n). Certain properties of this step response are worth learning: the initial rate of response is such that if continued the final value would be reached in exactly one-time constant. The actual function reaches 63% of its final value in one-time constant. Five-time constants are required to reach within 1.0%, seven for 0.1%, and ten for 0.01% accuracy; these numbers suggest the criterion of dynamic accuracy that is most used in practical design work.

If more gain or more speed or both are required, an amplifier with a greater gain-bandwidth product is one possibility. The other possibility is two or more operational circuits in cascade—but anyone with this kind of requirement either knows well what he is about or is radically mistaken about everything. If multiple circuits are used, the rule is that the errors of succeeding stages are divided by the signal gain of the circuits preceding them, which often means that only the input amplifier is critical as to the non-dynamic errors it introduces. These remarks apply to the response to *small* input signals, to which the circuit responds as a linear system. A 10-volt step evokes a nonlinear response not within the purview of this chapter.

The simple follower emerges from the analysis of Figure 10.11 if n is set equal to unity. Its characteristic frequency is equal to the gain-crossover frequency of the amplifier because its loop gain is the open-loop

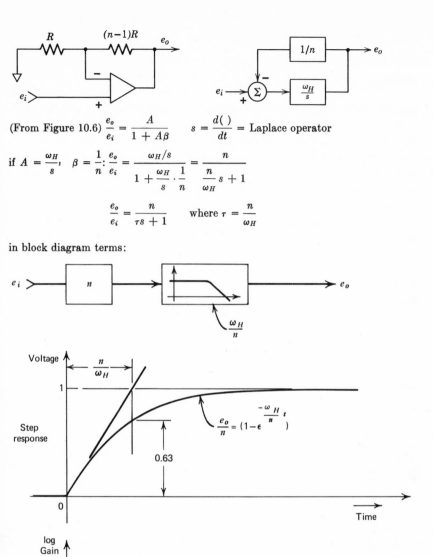

(From Figure 10.6) $\dfrac{e_o}{e_i} = \dfrac{A}{1 + A\beta}$ $\qquad s = \dfrac{d(\ )}{dt} = $ Laplace operator

if $A = \dfrac{\omega_H}{s}$, $\quad \beta = \dfrac{1}{n} : \dfrac{e_o}{e_i} = \dfrac{\omega_H/s}{1 + \dfrac{\omega_H}{s} \cdot \dfrac{1}{n}} = \dfrac{n}{\dfrac{n}{\omega_H} s + 1}$

$$\dfrac{e_o}{e_i} = \dfrac{n}{\tau s + 1} \qquad \text{where } \tau = \dfrac{n}{\omega_H}$$

in block diagram terms:

Figure 10.11. Dynamic analysis of follower-with-gain circuit of amplification factor n.

gain. By contrast, for the invertor, n = 2 and the bandwidth is one-half that of the follower, as rationalized immediately below.

The discussion of dynamic response has thus far treated follower circuits, but the argument is easily extended to inverting amplifiers. It was asserted in Chapter 4 that the invertor and the follower-with-gain of 2 were functionally identical; a further implication is that the invertor is really a circuit with a signal gain of 2—it is just that we arrange to split the gain into halves of opposite polarity. From this point of view it follows that the invertor has the same feedback factor β as the follower-with-gain of 2, even though it appears to have only half the signal gain; we recognize that the apparent gain deficit is really the price for changing the signal polarity. And so on for inverting amplifiers of whatever gain; the two circuits are compared in Figure 10.12

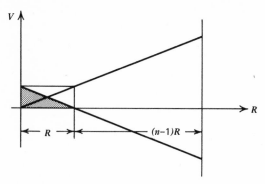

Figure 10.12.   Inverting and noninverting amplifiers made with generalized resistor ratio.

where it can be seen that the shaded area represents the sacrifice in signal amplification dictated by inversion. Thus, in matters affected by the feedback factor we can identify the inverting circuit with the correspondng follower circuit: the fractional error due to finite gain, the input voltage and current errors, the noise gain, the transient response, and as shown next, the sensitivity to load disturbances at the output—all are the same. There is nothing illusory about the contrast in input impedance, however.

One of the unquestioned triumphs of feedback systems and feedback amplifiers is their independence of load conditions. In comparison with systems innocent of feedback, *independent* is not too strong a word (provided that system ratings are not exceeded); yet a change in load has some effect, even if it is only transient. In the feedback arrangement two factors combine to minimize the effect of the disturbance. The first is the flow of information as to the actual output state back to the heart or nerve center of the system. This idea is now so familiar that *feedback* is in general misuse. The second factor is loop gain; the effect of a disturbance is divided by the gain in the closed loop. It is the *forward flow of power amplification,* and not just the backward flow of information, that puts the sting and snap into a feedback system.

It is a commonplace that "raw" output impedance is divided by the loop gain in a feedback circuit, and this paragraph should be skipped by those blinded by the self-evidence of the theorem. A typical micro-circuit operational amplifier has an output impedance of 3000 ohms; this means that the output behaves like a programmed voltage source responsive to the input difference voltage, and that there is an effective 3000-ohms resistance in series with the source. Figure 10.13 presents

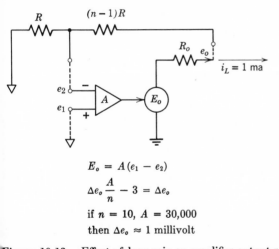

$$E_o = A(e_1 - e_2)$$

$$\Delta e_o \frac{A}{n} - 3 = \Delta e_o$$

if $n = 10$, $A = 30,000$

then $\Delta e_o \approx 1$ millivolt

Figure 10.13.   Effect of loop gain on amplifier output resistance.

this circuit model of the amplifier along with a feedback network having a feedback factor $\beta = 1/n$, representative of an invertor of gain $n - 1$ or a follower of gain n. If in the absence of feedback the output is called upon to deliver 1 milliampere to some sort of load (for example, a 15K-ohm resistor connected to the -15-volt supply when the output voltage is nominally zero), the result will be that the output voltage falls 3 volts due to the drop in the 3K-output resistance. In the presence of feedback let the output voltage drop under the load be Δe_o; $1/n$

of this drop will appear at the inverting input where it is inverted and amplified by the forward open-loop gain A_{dc}. Thus the programmed voltage source E_o shifts from zero to $+\Delta e_o\, A_{dc}/n$. If n is 10 and the gain is 30,000, then $E_o \approx +2.999$, and the output deflects about 1 millivolt under the load, as detailed by the little equation in the figure. The output is said to be *stiff* because of the *tight* loop closed around it. It is conventional and accurate to suppose that the output impedance has been literally divided by the loop gain A/n. Note, however, that if the signal gain were greater than 10 an error of more than 1 millivolt would be incurred, which would not do in a 10-volt 0.01% computer or instrumentation system. The same is true at frequencies where A is reduced by the rolloff of open-loop gain with frequency. Awareness of these matters is the requirement; they are easily disposed once identified.

An analogous argument shows that the input impedance of the amplifier is multiplied by the loop gain in the case of the follower. On this basis the follower-with-gain would have input impedance lowered in proportion to the signal gain. The reasoning is correct but irrelevant because as noted in Chapter 4 the input resistance of practical followers depends not on the bootstrapped differential mode impedance but on the common-mode resistance in parallel with it, which is impervious to manipulation by feedback.

A discussion of dynamic error may properly include the most radical error of all—output in the absence of input. Operational circuits, like all other feedback structures, oscillate vigorously if the feedback information is not both proper and *timely*. The importance of the second factor can be grasped from consideration of a novice driver steering in the direction of a skid but doing so too late each cycle and thus building a growing oscillation. The moral is that proper phase is of the essence for stable feedback systems. The 90° phase lag at all frequencies of the open-loop operational amplifier is so chosen because a loop with a single integrator as the only dynamic element cannot be unstable, cannot even exhibit an overshooting response to a step input, as the above results show. An integrator is an optimum open-loop characteristic to close a control loop around. Why? Why have any phase shift at all, or for that matter any signal attenuation? The answer is that without the attenuation of an integrator or other low-pass element, phase shift will accumulate due to parasitic effects until at some very high frequency there will be 180°, the gain will be greater than unity around the loop, and at that frequency there will be all hell breaking loose in a sustained oscillation. Negative feedback shifted 180° is explosively regenerative if the loop gain is greater than unity. The integrator rolloff assures that the phase will be only slightly greater than 90° when the gain falls to unity (which is a stable state of affairs), and that the gain will be safely below unity at that frequency for which the loop phase shift becomes 180°, and thus assures that regenerative action cannot occur. A well-known observation is that an amplifier is a poorly designed oscillator and vice versa. Indeed, operational circuits serve as admirable oscillators offering precise control of amplitude, frequency, and even phase of the generated signals. That, however, is remote from the present topic of the causes and cures of spurious instability.

The most frequent cause of the additional phase lag that engenders oscillation in operational circuits is capacitance from the summing point to ground. This capacitance, which is inherent between the inputs and from the inputs to ground in some small degree in all amplifiers, acting together with the feedback resistor (especially the larger values thereof), comprises a first-order lag that can contribute up to an additional 90° of phase, and cause trouble. Fortunately the cure is as easy as the cause is prevalent; it consists in adding a small feedback capacitor, so sized that the feedback network may be thought of as two equivalent voltage dividers in parallel, one resistive and one capacitive. See Figure 10.14.

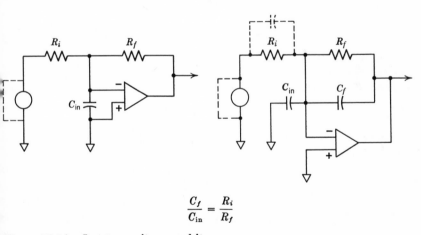

$$\frac{C_f}{C_{in}} = \frac{R_i}{R_f}$$

Figure 10.14. Input capacitance and its cure.

The result is called a phaseless divider and is much used in oscilloscope attenuators where stray capacitance is unavoidable but phase shift is absolute anathema. In practice it becomes second nature to add 10- to 100-picofarad feedback capacitance on general principles, sometimes much more if speed is no object and noise might be a nuisance. If speed is essential, one trims the feedback capacitor down experimentally (small variable radio capacitors turn out to be the right size range); if still more speed is needed, one adds a few picofarads across the input resistor, as shown dashed in the figure. A fast oscilloscope is needed for this kind of surgery.

The operational integrator circuit is never unstable in this way because it already has a capacitor as the feedback element. But the differentiator in the pure form given in Chapter 3 is *a priori unstable* because the feedback network is a pure lag and usually a very low-frequency one.

The operational integrator circuit deserves separate treatment here because of the possible confusion between the integration of signals and the integration incorporated into the open-loop response of the amplifier itself. The technique of dynamic analysis above is applied to the integrator circuit; the only new element is that the feedback factor β is frequency dependent. Figure 10.15 is the Bode plot of the integrator. Observe that the signal gain line is parallel to the open-loop gain in the middle and high frequencies, and several decades below it. Consequently, the loop gain represented by the hatched area is high enough for high accuracy over a wide frequency range—here one graph reveals the unique strength of the electronic differential analyzer. A typical value for the RC time constant of the integrator is 1 second, which means that the signal gain is unity at 1 radian per second, some seven decades below the gain crossover of a typical amplifier. Even an integrator scaled 1000-times faster has ample gain over a wide frequency span. Integrators run out of gain just as do followers on the high-frequency end, but this is seldom a problem. They also run out of gain in the range of ultraslow signals; the combination of rising signal gain and fixed dc gain of the amplifier means that the loop gain falls with frequency on the extreme low end. The practical result of this condition is that the integrator output decays slowly toward zero instead of holding constant during periods of zero input signal. If this sort of error is intolerable, a chopper-stabilized amplifier provides three or more decades of additional dc gain. This amplifier type would probably be used anyway for such long term integration. An expedient alternative is the use of positive feedback to boost the low-frequency gain, but this is a technique best suited to laboratory work. In ordinary computation and simulation this error source is not a problem.

The feedback network of the integrator is a lead network with characteristic frequency $1/RC$. Its gain is unity above this frequency and falls directly with frequency below it. The expression, $1/\beta$ is the noise gain and is equal to the signal gain below the characteristic frequency

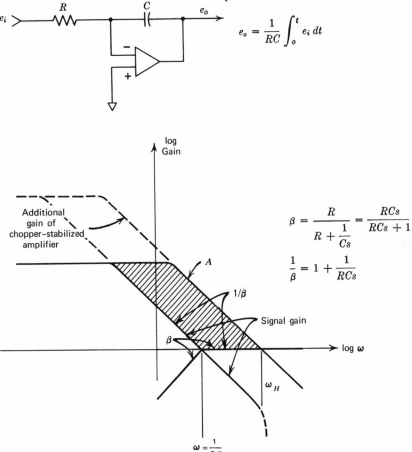

$$e_o = \frac{1}{RC} \int_o^t e_i \, dt$$

$$\beta = \frac{R}{R + \frac{1}{Cs}} = \frac{RCs}{RCs + 1}$$

$$\frac{1}{\beta} = 1 + \frac{1}{RCs}$$

Figure 10.15. Integrator-circuit dynamic analysis.

and to unity above it. The integrator and the follower are alike in their high-frequency noise gain, which is sensible when one reflects that at high frequency the feedback capacitor becomes a very low impedance, very much like a piece of copper wire. In both of these circuits the amplifier is said to be tightly fed back, which means that the loop gain at high frequency is high. This is a severe test of the amplifier stability. If the amplifier suffers from additional phase (more than 90°) as its gain crosses unity, there will be ringing in the transient response of these circuits—an effect invariably puzzling to the relative neophyte who associates ringing with inductors rather than marginally stable feedback structures.

Chapter XI

Instrumentation

The importance of an apt name for a new circuit configuration was touched on in Chapter 2; a related problem is the categorization of circuits. Clear thinking does not produce a satisfying classification for every circuit, due in part to the underlying unity of the subject. The definitions below guide the organization of the balance of the book:

A circuit that extracts information from its surroundings is an instrumentation circuit.

A circuit that refines information or generates it is a computation circuit; it need not be strongly coupled to its surroundings.

The quandary of classification is well illustrated by the Absolute Value Amplifier of Figure 11.1. It could easily belong in the computation chapter in view of its precision and the mathematical salience of the operation. It is here because its follower input and wide dynamic range qualify it for instrument service. It is also here because of a quibble: the output is the absolute value of the input multiplied by a constant greater than unity.

This circuit is not placed first because of its simplicity, although its two modes are not difficult to understand or even much different from each other; they are shown separately in Figure 11.2, which may obviate further explication. For positive inputs the upper amplifier is a follower-with-gain; the lower amplifier provides a ground reference for the feedback network because it is tightly fed back through the low resistance of the conducting diode. In the language of Chapter 6 the lower amplifier

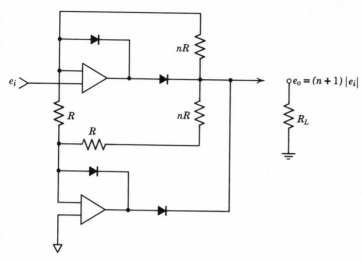

Figure 11.1.   High-impedance absolute value amplifier.

is zero-bounded. That is, like all well-brought-up and well-fedback differential amplifiers it keeps its inputs together in voltage (subject to the microscopic aberrations disclosed in Chapter 9). Alternatively stated, it behaves like a voltage follower with zero input, its output terminal swinging about 0.6-volt negative to draw off the computing network current through the diode and maintain the voltage null across the inputs. For negative inputs the upper amplifier becomes a similar unity-gain follower transferring the signal to the inverting amplifier

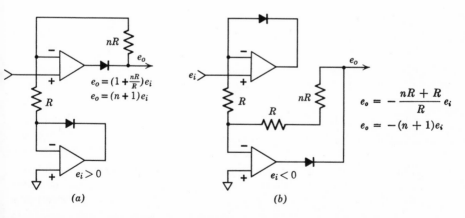

Figure 11.2.   Functional dissection of Figure 11.1. (a) $e_i > 0$ and (b) $e_i < 0$.

circuit below. The outputs are summed together by confluence in the manner of Figure 6.20, which as the precursor of this circuit should be reexamined at this time.

This absolute-value circuit is a fair one-circuit review of the preceding ten chapters. Note that the voltage error magnification factor is $(n+1)$ for positive inputs and $(n+2)$ for negative inputs. Various tolerancing or matching strategies can be applied to the resistors to achieve a variety of cost versus accuracy objectives.

The Difference Amplifier of Chapter 5, for all of its power and symmetric glory, does not have high-resistance inputs, not at least of the sort provided by follower configurations. One finds himself wishing for a differential form of the follower, having two high-resistance inputs and one low-resistance output proportional to the input difference voltage, and utterly indifferent to the common-mode voltage. It is a reasonable wish, in fact it is a description of what has come to be called an Instrumentation Amplifier. Two followers driving the inputs of a Difference Amplifier have been used, and although the force is brute the performance is brilliant, and much of the world's aerospace and industrial data are gathered by circuits like that in Figure 11.3. Three

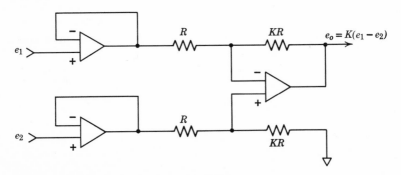

Figure 11.3. Basic instrumentation amplifier.

additional resistors enable a very significant refinement of the basic circuit into the form of Figure 11.4. This circuit is of unmatched importance from several points of view. Note that if the inputs are tied together and driven with a signal, the circuit reduces to a simple follower or to *two* simple followers in superposed parallel. This demonstrates that the common-mode gain is unity, which analysis confirms. See Figure 11.5. The analysis uses the principle that the inputs must stay together

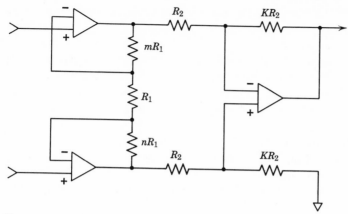

Figure 11.4.   Cross-coupled differential follower-with-gain instrumentation amplifier.

to get at the individual output voltages, which are then subtracted to give the differential-mode gain.

Note well:

1. The feedback network need not be balanced.

2. Differential signals are amplified, yet common-mode signals are passed at unity gain.

Thus, even though this circuit does not literally reject common-mode signals, it does have a differential-mode-to-common-mode amplification

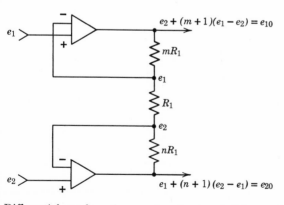

Differential mode $\rightarrow (e_{20} - e_{10}) = (m + n + 1)(e_2 - e_1)$

Common mode $\rightarrow \dfrac{e_{20} + e_{10}}{2} = \dfrac{e_2 + e_1}{2}$

Figure 11.5.   Cross-coupled differential follower-with-gain.

ratio equal to the differential-mode gain. The circuit thus may be said to possess a common-mode rejection ratio or CMRR; this effect, though relative, is very real, for the CMRR of this stage multiplies that of the difference amplifier to give the superb overall rejection ratio. It is perfectly reasonable to measure differences to better than one part per million. The difference amplifier carries its CMRR in the form of a nominal differential-mode gain and a great common-mode attenuation, and thus handles the job of erasing the common-mode component from the final output. But with the gain and hence the CMRR of the cross-coupled follower in front of it, which can easily be as much as 1000, even a mediocre difference amplifier can do a splendid job. This circuit is a remarkable tribute to a technology. A marriage of this configuration with a differential form of low-pass Butterworth signal filter is given later in this chapter as a highly evolved data-acquisition amplifier, accompanied by some remarks about the service environment that forced its evolution.

The original dream of a more or less simple follower with differential inputs remains tantalizing. The amplifier itself has two inputs and it seems as if there should be a way . . . and there is. See Figure 11.6.

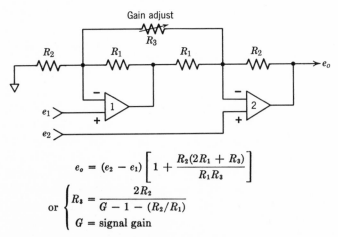

$$e_o = (e_2 - e_1)\left[1 + \frac{R_2(2R_1 + R_3)}{R_1 R_3}\right]$$

$$\text{or} \begin{cases} R_3 = \dfrac{2R_2}{G - 1 - (R_2/R_1)} \\ G = \text{signal gain} \end{cases}$$

Figure 11.6.   Differential follower-with-gain.

It uses two amplifiers but uses them to the full. This elegant circuit was shown to me by R. A. Pease of Philbrick/Nexus, who is responsible for the gain-ranging feature, which has apparently not been published.

Assuming initially that the gain-ranging resistor R_3 is absent, the circuit may be regarded as two coupled followers-with-gain. If e_2 is zero, the second amplifier becomes a simple inverting amplifier of gain R_2/R_1; it operates on the output of the first amplifier which is a follower of gain $1 + R_1/R_2$; the complete gain is thus:

$$\left(1 + \frac{R_1}{R_2}\right)\left(-\frac{R_2}{R_1}\right) = -\left(\frac{R_2}{R_1} + 1\right)$$

If e_1 is zero, the output of amplifier 1 is also zero, and amplifier 2 is a follower of gain $1 + R_2/R_1$. For equal inputs the output is zero, as shown by the V-R diagram in Figure 11.7. The accuracy and common-mode rejection are critically dependent upon the resistor accuracy,

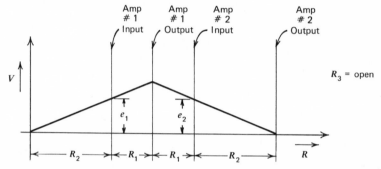

Figure 11.7. Common-mode rejection mechanism of differential follower.

and the easiest course is to employ very high accuracy components, rather than to attempt matching or triming. The common-mode rejection is completely independent of R_3, which may be conveniently switched to values computed from the equation in Figure 11.6 for a very wide range of calibrated gains, or which may be made variable for adjustable gain. Resistor R_3 carries a current proportional to the input difference $(e_2 - e_1)$ away from the inverting input of amplifier 2. An equal current is carried away by resistor R_1 because of the inversion in amplifier 1; thus R_3 has a direct and an indirect effect both of which increase the signal gain. The circuit action is by far the most intricate of any in this book, yet the result is rewarding both practically and aesthetically.

The same intercoupled configuration can be exploited to make a differential current follower. The basic circuit has been presented in Chapter 9, but is repeated here for comparison with its voltage counterpart. See

Figure 11.8. Resistor R_3 is omitted because there is no voltage difference to cause current to flow in it. The omission is suggestive, however; a similar one-element gain control can be devised: resistor R_4 serves this purpose in accordance with the equation given in the figure. To the experienced eye, two inverting amplifiers in a loop like the one formed by R_4 signify positive feedback. Indeed, R_4 provides positive feedback that opposes the conventional negative feedback by R_1 and R_2 and thus increases the signal gain. As long as R_4 is larger than R_2 the overall feedback is negative and all is well. The equation in the figure is eloquent of what happens when R_4 becomes equal to R_2.

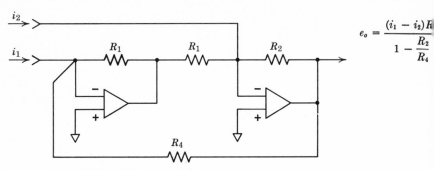

$$e_o = \frac{(i_1 - i_2)R}{1 - \dfrac{R_2}{R_4}}$$

Figure 11.8.   Differential current follower.

The differential voltage follower is a true ideal voltmeter. Within the limits of the common-mode range and output swing of the amplifiers it is a high-resistance instrument sensitive only to potential difference. No similar capability can be claimed by the differential current follower above because it can measure only currents flowing to ground. A simple current meter or a current follower with a power supply of its own is said to float. A floating meter has three properties that must be provided in the design of a nonfloating circuit in order for it to be equivalent: (1) the meter is independent of voltage level, (2) there are no current paths from either terminal of the meter circuit to ground or to any other point, and (3) current is conserved in the meter circuit—the current entering one terminal of the meter circuit is instantaneously identical with that leaving the other. One circuit that has these attributes consists of a current-sampling resistor measured by a differential voltage follower. See Figure 11.9. Unfortunately a 1-ohm sampling resistor provides only 1 microvolt per microampere, which is hopelessly down in the voltage uncertainty of even the best operational amplifier. In short, the sampling resistor is an approach but not a very close one. A truly floating differential current follower is required but has proven very elusive. The circuit of Figure 11.10 appears to be such a specimen.

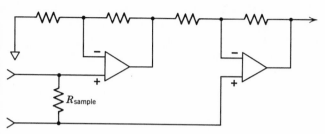

Figure 11.9. Sampling resistor approach to a floating current-meter circuit.

The circuit of Figure 11.10 is the functional dual of Figure 11.5, with which it should be carefully compared. This is the first application of a true differential-input, differential-output, high-gain composite operational amplifier, the configuration within the dashed lines. The common mode of the outputs is set by conventional follower action, whereas

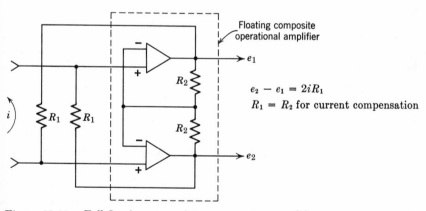

Figure 11.10. Full-floating zero-resistance current preamplifier.

the differential-mode negative feedback is achieved by cross-coupling. Current compensation in the manner of Chapter 9 is inherent in the configuration because the value of R_2 can always be chosen to accomplish it. Like the simple current follower this circuit is prone to sizable error when the signal source resistance is low. In particular, 1 millivolt of amplifier voltage error is indistinguishable from 1 microampere of current from a source of 1000-ohms resistance. This is not really a circuit limitation so much as a consequence of the measurement of an ultralow energy source (1 microampere and 1 kilohm is only one billionth of a watt). A difference amplifier is indicated if a single-ended voltage signal is the desired output.

Signal filters are frequency-sensitive networks of which the most familiar examples are the tone controls of entertainment equipment. Filter design has always been a specialty within the electrical engineering profession because it requires a degree of mathematical literacy approaching that of the applied mathematician. Active filters implemented with operational amplifiers are a good deal easier to understand but are still beyond the scope of this book as direct subject matter. However, a complete data amplifier and filter are given as an example of how functions may opportunistically be combined and also to illustrate how a differential form of a network is fashioned from a single-ended prototype, without altering the mathematics of its response. The amplifier configuration is the Instrumentation Amplifier of Figure 11.4. The filter is a third-order low-pass Butterworth as given in 3.23(b), p. 75 of the Philbrick/Nexus *Applications Manual for Operational Amplifiers* (see Figure 11.11). The amplitude response of the filter is unity below the cutoff frequency, $1/RC$ radians per second, and falls inversely with the cube of the frequency above cutoff. The construction and testing of this filter in its single-ended form is impressively educational for those unfamiliar with this kind of hardware.

The task of the data amplifier is to extract a low-level (10-millivolt full scale) low-frequency (5 hertz and below) differential-mode signal in the presence of differential-mode pickup, principally at power-line frequency and its harmonics, as well as dc and above common-mode voltages, again principally related to the power line. Thus the following functions are required: preamplification, filtering, common-mode rejection, double-ended-to-single-ended conversion, and final amplification (scaling). Simply cascading the instrumentation amplifier of Figure 11.4 or 11.6 with the filter of Figure 11.11 will do a creditable job. The limitation is that the differential-mode pickup can be much larger than the data signal and can saturate the amplifier unless filtering precedes final amplification. Thus after the cross-coupled follower preamplifier and before the difference amplifier of Figure 11.4 would be an ideal place for the filter. The filter must, however, operate *only* on *differential-mode* signals, because any filtering of the common mode ahead of the difference amplifier must be absolutely balanced; unbalanced filtering transduces common-mode voltages into spurious differential mode signals. Because *volts* of common mode are usually present the only balanced filtering is zero filtering. These considerations lead to the configuration of Figure 11.12. The portion of the filter to the left of the summing

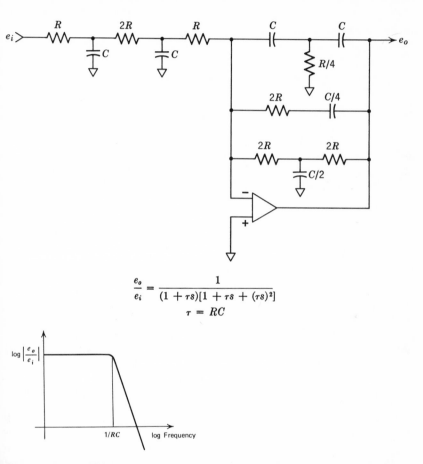

$$\frac{e_o}{e_i} = \frac{1}{(1 + \tau s)[1 + \tau s + (\tau s)^2]}$$

$$\tau = RC$$

Figure 11.11.   Third-order low-pass butterworth filter. (Taken from Philbrick/ Nexus, *Applications Manual for Operational Amplifiers*, p. 75.

point in Figure 11.11 was recognized as a low-pass unbalanced ladder network. It was balanced by splitting the resistors, and the resulting structure used to replace the input resistors of the difference amplifier. In a very real sense the filtering operation is orthogonal to the common-mode voltage. Just as the original network was driven by the signal

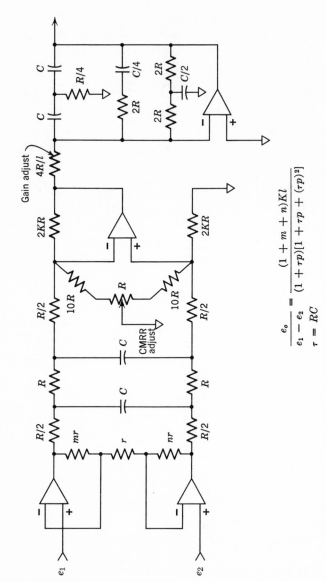

Figure 11.12. Data acquisition amplifier and filter.

$$\frac{e_o}{e_1 - e_2} = \frac{(1 + m + n)Kl}{(1 + \tau p)[1 + \tau p + (\tau p)^2]}$$

$$\tau = RC$$

voltage source and connected to a summing point, so is the balanced version driven by the outputs of the differential follower and connected to the voltage null of the difference amplifier input terminals. The feedback elements of the filter perform conventionally to shape the response in a mathematically predetermined way, thus giving the flatness of response in the pass band for which the Butterworth filter is noted. The common-mode rejection is easily adjusted to better than one-million-to-one with the potentiometer shown. The procedure is to drive both inputs with a low-frequency signal and adjust for zero output. Gain is adjusted conveniently by the resistor shown.

Chopper-stabilized amplifiers have unequaled long-term voltage stability but are single-ended and thus restricted to inverting configurations. An exception to the foregoing is that stabilized followers, unity-gain only, of superb performance become possible if the chopper-stabilized amplifier can have its own floating power supply—the manufacturer can advise. The next circuit is an inverting preamplifier with its input resistance augmented by means of a parallel feedback bootstrapping scheme. It uses a chopper-stabilized main amplifier with an auxiliary amplifier (perhaps a microcircuit type) which provides the impedance boosting feedback. See Figure 11.13. This is workable because the voltage

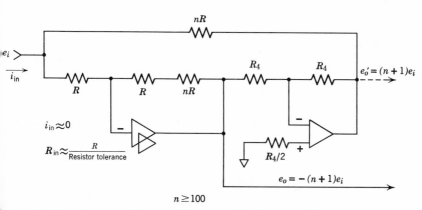

Figure 11.13. Augmented-input resistance-stabilized preamplifier.

uncertainty of the second amplifier is divided by the signal gain preceding it, which should be one hundred or more for this scheme to work properly. The effective input resistance is raised in proportion to the precision of the resistors used throughout. If desired the bootstrapping resistor may be trimmed by adjusting it for minimum loading of a high-resistance test signal source. The inverting output is the most accurate, but the other may be used if the signal voltage level is high compared with the voltage error of the auxiliary amplifier, and if the resistors R_4 are precisely matched. If R is 10K, n is 100, and the resistor tolerance is 0.01%, an input resistance on the order of 100 megohms may be expected. This is not follower performance, but taken with the voltage stability of the chopper amplifier and the freedom from input *current* error, the circuit has its uses. Interestingly enough the effective input resistance can be negative if the resistor tolerances are such that over-compensation of the input-signal current takes place. This should cause no more than momentary consternation because whether input resistance is negative or positive matters not at all provided only that it is *large*. Put another way, when the input resistance is large and negative the signal source holds back on the amplifier circuit, as a drover would a peculiar mule who tended to go—but very feebly.

Ac amplifiers are by no means simply "DC amplifiers with blocking capacitors," to rebut an early and otherwise admirable manufacturer's handbook; on the contrary they are among the operational circuits most demanding of the designer's skill. The reasons are that dc paths must

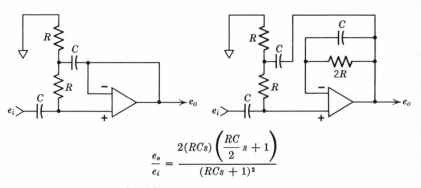

$$\frac{e_o}{e_i} = \frac{2(RCs)\left(\dfrac{RC}{2}s + 1\right)}{(RCs + 1)^2}$$

Figure 11.14.   Ac-coupled follower.

be provided for the input error currents, and a dc feedback structure must be arranged to maintain the circuit at a nominal equilibrium state ready to handle the ac information. Both must be done without degrading the input impedance and other characteristics. The ac voltage follower is a case in point. How does one provide a dc path to the positive input of a capacitively coupled follower without compromising its input resistance? The answer is an ac bootstrap technique. See Figure 11.14

The input current for the direct input flows through the resistive network whose centerpoint is bootstrapped by the capacitor connected to the output terminal. A substantial dc offset results that may be objectionable if the full output voltage swing is required. A bypassed compensation resistor is ameliorative in the unity-gain case, as shown at the right of the figure, but for followers-with-gain a fundamental problem exists:

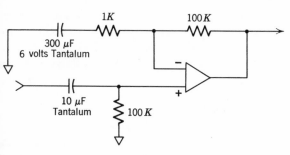

Figure 11.15. Ac follower-with-gain with unity gain for dc offset errors.

how is it possible to build a follower of arbitrary gain for ac signals, yet small gain for its own voltage and current errors? A conventional approach is to decouple the gain-setting feedback network from ground at low frequency by means of a large capacitor, as shown in Figure 11.15. The simplicity is attractive but the cost and volume of the capacitor are not, and the example shown is at the practical limit of capacitance value. The alternative shown in Figure 11.16 is such that the entire volume of the circuit is comparable to that of a microcircuit amplifier

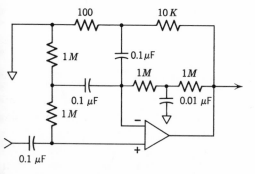

Figure 11.16. Ac-bootstrapped ac-coupled follower-with-gain.

if ceramic capacitors are used. The dc feedback and the input current for the inverting input are provided by the high-resistance network, which is decoupled above a minimal frequency by the capacitor to ground. This allows the ac gain to be set by a customary feedback network capacitively coupled to the inverting input. The input resistor network is ac bootstrapped as before. The principal output offset for a transistor amplifier is caused by net input error current flowing in the high-resistance biasing networks. These resistors must be large for a given capacitor because they control the lower-cutoff frequency of the amplifier. The upper-cutoff frequency is caused by the rolloff of the amplifier itself unless it is further restricted by additional components.

One of the motives for ac coupling is to eliminate unwanted constant components of the data which may be much larger than the phenomena of interest. Particularly in geophysical data the interest may center in the fine structure of small perturbations about monumental nominal values. However, the perturbations though small are not necessarily rapid and in fact often contain dc components that should be preserved. For this and other reasons conventional ac coupling is sometimes a poor approach to what is really a zero or base-line suppression problem. An extreme form of ac coupling applies directly here; it has been made practical by the minute input current errors of parametric operational amplifiers and by the high quality of polystyrene capacitors. See Figure 11.17. The switch is momentarily closed at the beginning of an experi-

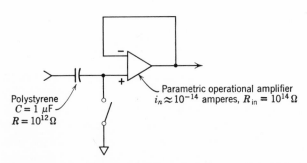

Figure 11.17.   Zero-suppression circuit (ac coupling with dc response).

ment, thus storing the unwanted initial value as charge on the capacitor. Thereafter, if the capacitor is 1 microfarad, frequencies as low as 10^{-6} radian per second are passed without attenuation. The output voltage drifts at a rate of 10^{-8} volt per second due to the amplifier error current.

Figure 11.18 illustrates the Tee network of resistors in the most important of its several applications. In this network, resistors of ordinary values simulate a resistor of exotically high value. As illustrated, resistors R_2 and R_3 form a voltage divider that reduces the voltage applied to R_f and thus raises its effective value proportionately. This scheme is

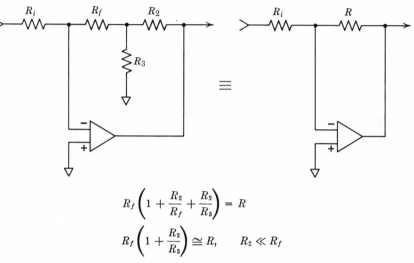

$$R_f\left(1 + \frac{R_2}{R_f} + \frac{R_2}{R_3}\right) = R$$

$$R_f\left(1 + \frac{R_2}{R_3}\right) \cong R, \qquad R_2 \ll R_f$$

Figure 11.18. Principle of the Tee network.

useful for increasing the signal gain of an inverting amplifier—provided, as will be shown below, that the ratio R_f/R_i is substantial before the voltage divider is applied. When this condition is not met the voltage noise gain of the circuit becomes so large that it is unacceptable in many applications. This is a consequence of the algebra of cascaded voltage dividers and is one of the effects that made a mockery of the attempted fix chronicled in Chapter 9. The ratio of the signal and noise gains of this circuit is given in Figure 11.19. It is clear enough that the two gains become essentially equal when R_f/R_i is large compared with unity.

The effect of the Tee network is identical to that of the large resistor it emulates, in regard to errors due to input current. The disastrous example of Chapter 9 makes this amply clear.

Figure 11.20 illustrates the application of Tee networks to the augmented input-resistance circuit, a principal limitation of which is the unavailability of precise resistors above 1 megohm. In the modified circuit two identical dividers magnify both the effective feedback resistor and the effective parallel bootstrapping resistor. Tee networks must work into virtual grounds to operate correctly, and it appears that the bootstrap network in Figure 11.20 connects not to a virtual ground but to the signal source. But if the input resistor R is considered to be part

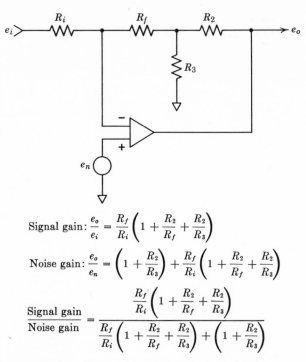

$$\text{Signal gain:} \frac{e_o}{e_i} = \frac{R_f}{R_i}\left(1 + \frac{R_2}{R_f} + \frac{R_2}{R_3}\right)$$

$$\text{Noise gain:} \frac{e_o}{e_n} = \left(1 + \frac{R_2}{R_3}\right) + \frac{R_f}{R_i}\left(1 + \frac{R_2}{R_f} + \frac{R_2}{R_3}\right)$$

$$\frac{\text{Signal gain}}{\text{Noise gain}} = \frac{\dfrac{R_f}{R_i}\left(1 + \dfrac{R_2}{R_f} + \dfrac{R_2}{R_3}\right)}{\dfrac{R_f}{R_i}\left(1 + \dfrac{R_2}{R_f} + \dfrac{R_2}{R_3}\right) + \left(1 + \dfrac{R_2}{R_3}\right)}$$

Figure 11.19.   Noise analysis of tee-network amplifier.

of the bootstrap Tee network, it is seen that both networks are identical and that both connect to the summing point of the chopper-stabilized amplifier. Thus only the tiny transient currents dictated by causality flow to and from the signal source, the equilibrium loop currents being supplied—in principle exactly—by the auxiliary amplifier through the Tee network. As before, resistor accuracy is crucial to high-input resistance. An illustrative design given in the figure uses 0.01% resistors to give a gain of 1000 and an input resistance approaching 1000 megohms.

Tee networks are germane to the design of high-resolution resistance readout circuits. This subject was briefly introduced at the close of Chapter 7, the last three paragraphs of which should be reviewed before proceeding.

The circuit of Figure 7.14 provides a known current through the resistor under test and produces an output voltage equal to the product of this current and the resistive deviation or increment. Unfortunately,

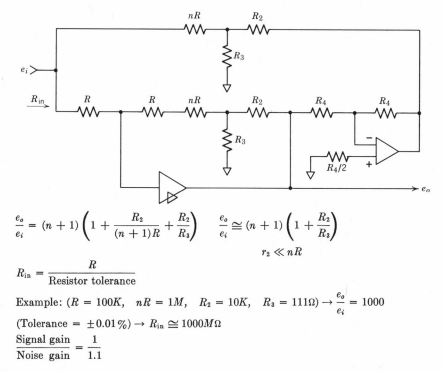

$$\frac{e_o}{e_i} = (n + 1)\left(1 + \frac{R_2}{(n + 1)R} + \frac{R_2}{R_3}\right) \qquad \frac{e_o}{e_i} \cong (n + 1)\left(1 + \frac{R_2}{R_3}\right)$$

$$r_2 \ll nR$$

$$R_{in} = \frac{R}{\text{Resistor tolerance}}$$

Example: $(R = 100K, \quad nR = 1M, \quad R_2 = 10K, \quad R_3 = 111\Omega) \rightarrow \dfrac{e_o}{e_i} = 1000$

$(\text{Tolerance} = \pm 0.01\%) \rightarrow R_{in} \cong 1000M\Omega$

$$\frac{\text{Signal gain}}{\text{Noise gain}} = \frac{1}{1.1}$$

Figure 11.20. Tee networks applied to augmented-input resistance preamplifier.

this Ohm's law product signal is in no way amplified. For high-resolution measurements the signal perforce is small, and a means of making the circuit amplify this signal is needed for several reasons, not the least of which is the cost of a second amplifier of noise performance equaling the first. Enter the Tee network.

The basic circuit is shown in Figure 11.21. The unknown is in the feedback as before, but with a voltage divider between it and the output terminal. The circuit as drawn omits all provision for making the zero of resistive deviation correspond with zero-volts output, an important problem that the differential circuit solves automatically. As drawn, the output would be wildly offscale, but that is not an immediate concern. Analysis reveals that the circuit differs markedly from the Tee network voltage amplifier. See Figure 11.19. The difference arises from the unusual location of the effective signal source, since unlike conventional

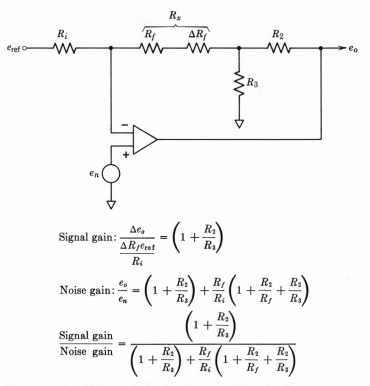

Signal gain: $\dfrac{\Delta e_o}{\dfrac{\Delta R_f e_{\text{ref}}}{R_i}} = \left(1 + \dfrac{R_2}{R_3}\right)$

Noise gain: $\dfrac{e_o}{e_n} = \left(1 + \dfrac{R_2}{R_3}\right) + \dfrac{R_f}{R_i}\left(1 + \dfrac{R_2}{R_f} + \dfrac{R_2}{R_3}\right)$

$\dfrac{\text{Signal gain}}{\text{Noise gain}} = \dfrac{\left(1 + \dfrac{R_2}{R_3}\right)}{\left(1 + \dfrac{R_2}{R_3}\right) + \dfrac{R_f}{R_i}\left(1 + \dfrac{R_2}{R_f} + \dfrac{R_2}{R_3}\right)}$

Figure 11.21.   Noise analysis of resistance readout circuit.

signal and noise sources it is an effective voltage source in series with the *feedback* path. The expressions for signal gain and for noise gain (unchanged) and for their ratio are given in the figure. Once more the two gains approach each other, this time for small values of R_f/R_i—a rather remarkable result.

Since R_f is given, one chooses the reference resistor R_i and thus the reference source e_{ref} to be as large as possible. A current source would be ideal, resulting in identical signal and noise gains (a clear optimum) but in practice a value $R_i = 10R_f$ will usually be adequate. Considerations of the accuracy of the reference source should inform the choice of R_i. In this connection it should be kept in mind that the two most used voltage standards are the saturated standard cell at about 1 volt and the zener reference diode at about 8 volts. It is essential that ultrastable resistors be used in circuitry intended to measure a shift of resistance on the order of one part per million, as are the circuits to follow. The so-called thick-film resistors having temperature coefficients of 1 ppm/°C are highly recommended.

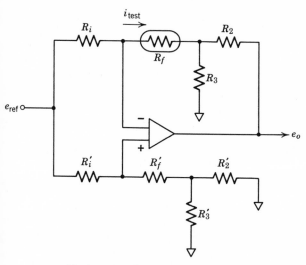

Design procedure:

Given: R_f, $\Delta R_{f\,max}$, i_{test}, $e_{o\,max}$

Choose: $e_{ref} > 10 i_{test} R_f$

Then follow design routine

Design routine:

1. $R_3 = \dfrac{R_f}{10}$

2. $R_2 = \left(\dfrac{e_{o\,max}}{i_{test}\,\Delta R_{f\,max}} - 1 \right) \dfrac{R_f}{10}$

3. $R_i = \dfrac{e_{ref}}{i_{test}} - R_f - \dfrac{R_2 R_3}{R_2 + R_3}$

Figure 11.22. High-resolution resistance deviation readout using differential amplifier.

The final form of the circuit for use with a differential amplifier is given in Figure 11.22 along with a design procedure. Certain chopper-stabilized amplifiers can be used in this circuit by treating a terminal variously labeled "signal ground" or "high-quality ground" as the direct input, or can be easily modified by the manufacturer so that they can be so applied. In fact, such amplifiers can be used quite generally in differential circuits, provided that the common-mode voltage does not change rapidly (perhaps 1 volt per second or less). Since in this circuit the common-mode voltage is constant there is literally no problem. When such an amplifier is available this is unquestionably the circuit of choice.

An incidental but significant advantage of the Tee network is that the amplifier output does not have to absorb the test current, most of which flows to ground through R_3. For low-resistance unknowns this current may be sizeable.

Before leaving the differential circuit of Figure 11.22, it should be observed that several such circuits can be served by one high-quality reference voltage source. Reference current can be conserved by making the primed resistors some convenient multiple of their unprimed counterparts.

If a single-ended amplifier must be used, the problem of returning the output voltage to zero, or even of keeping it on scale, is most difficult. A solution of sorts uses dual plus and minus reference sources such as reference grade operational power supplies. See Figure 11.23. The circuit is critically dependent on the tracking accuracy of the dual refer-ences. This means the degree to which the reference voltages depart from being mirror images. Quantitatively, the tracking error is simply the algebraic sum of the two reference voltages. Step 7 of the design procedure in the figure enables the influence of tracking error on circuit error to be evaluated. It will usually be found that the tracking error dominates to such a degree that the use of a chopper-stabilized amplifier is questionable.

If a second amplifier is used the reference tracking error can be sub-tracted out, as shown in Figure 11.24. This scheme provides for the differential measurement of a pair of resistive transducers. If, for exam-ple, the transducers are resistance strain gages mounted on opposite sides of a beam in bending, the resulting instrument measures bending strain but is unaffected by tension or compression. This arrangement can approach the dynamic range of the strain gage, which is on the order of 10^7. Usually a digital voltmeter or another instrument having differential inputs is the next equipment in a system of this kind, so that the cost of the implied differential-to-single-ended conversion is neither direct nor large.

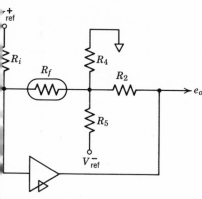

Design procedure:

1. $R_i = \dfrac{V_{\text{ref}}}{i_{\text{test}}}$ $R_i > 10R_f$

2. $R_2 = \dfrac{R_f}{10}\left(\dfrac{e_{o\,\text{max}}}{i_{\text{test}}\,\Delta R_{f\,\text{max}}} - 1\right)$

3. $q = \left[1 + \dfrac{1}{10}\left(1 + \dfrac{R_f}{R_2}\right)\right]i_{\text{test}}R_f$

4. $R_4 = \left(\dfrac{q}{V_{\text{ref}} - q} + 1\right)\dfrac{R_f}{10}$

5. $R_5 = \dfrac{\dfrac{R_f}{10}R_4}{\left(R_4 - \dfrac{R_f}{10}\right)}$

6. Signal gain: $\dfrac{e_o}{\Delta R_f} = \dfrac{V_{\text{ref}}}{R_i}\left(1 + 10\dfrac{R_2}{R_f}\right)$

7. Reference tracking error: $\Delta e_o = 10\dfrac{R_2}{R_i}(\Delta V_{\text{ref}}^+ + \Delta V_{\text{ref}}^-)$

8. Voltage noise gain: $\dfrac{e_o}{e_n} = \left(1 + 10\dfrac{R_2}{R_f}\right) + \dfrac{R_f}{R_i}\left(1 + \dfrac{R_2}{R_f} + 10\dfrac{R_2}{R_f}\right)$

Figure 11.23. High-resolution resistance readout with single-ended amplifier and dual-tracking references.

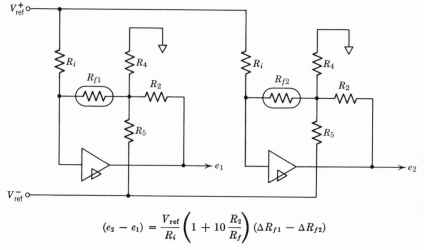

$$(e_2 - e_1) = \frac{V_{\text{ref}}}{R_i}\left(1 + 10\,\frac{R_2}{R_f}\right)(\Delta R_{f1} - \Delta R_{f2})$$

Figure 11.24. Differential high-resolution resistance readout.

If a single measurement is to be made it is best to use the additional chopper-stabilized amplifier as an invertor to create what is, in effect, a negative reference voltage. Figure 11.25 shows how this is managed when one of the power supplies for the operational amplifiers is used as the reference, as will frequently be the case. The trick is to use some voltage within the amplifier swing capability, for example, 10 volts, as the reference voltage V_{ref} in designing the circuit by the procedure

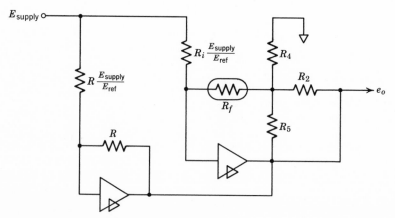

Figure 11.25. Modification of Figure 11.23.

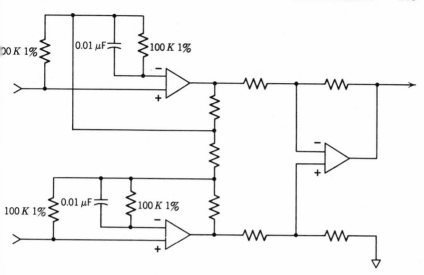

Figure 11.26. Instrumentation amplifier with current compensation (see Figure 11.4).

of Figure 11.23, and then to scale R_i and the other input resistor as shown in Figure 11.25.

All of these circuits can be made to work for the conductance case corresponding to Figure 7.16. The same remarks apply with this exception: from a noise standpoint the conductance case is the same as the amplifier of Figure 11.19, that is, a large value of R_f/R_i is indicated.

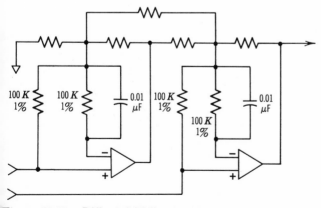

Figure 11.27. Differential follower with current compensation (see Figure 11.6).

A very simple means of current compensation is described briefly at the close of Chapter 9. Although it looks at first like the most disastrous kind of positive feedback, it is not. It enables transistor amplifiers to be used with much higher source resistances than are otherwise practicable. Figures 11.26 and 11.27 show this method applied to the two instrumentation amplifiers presented earlier in this chapter.

Chapter XII

Computation

This chapter, like the preceding one, begins with an absolute-value circuit; this mathematical function, which appears so amenable to nonlinear operational technique, has become a classical problem in the field. The implementation shown in Figure 12.1 is something of a rarity—a dual-mode circuit that is completely balanced in each mode, both for diode voltages and amplifier input currents. For negative inputs an invertor mode obtains with D_2, coupling the direct input to ground while D_1 blocks. Positive inputs invoke follower action through D_1 with the feedback network behaving as a two-to-one voltage divider, referenced not to ground but to the input signal. Thus the signal gain is unity, but the loop gain and bandwidth are the same as in the inverter mode—even the dynamic response is the same in the two modes. The $5K$ resistor balances the feedback network both in regard to input current compensation and in regard to the currents in the conducting diodes, which currents are not constant but are always closely balanced. The circuit uses the principle that diodes matched as to forward voltage at a given current match also at other currents in the vicinity. The conducting diodes in this circuit always operate at 100 microamperes or more, which accounts for the notable speed of the circuit, approaching that of the corresponding invertor. Because both the diodes D_1 and D_2 partially conduct near zero input there is significant rounding error within about 50 millivolts of the origin of the input-output characteristic, as shown in the figure. An accuracy of 0.1% of full scale (10 volts) is reasonable elsewhere, using diodes matched to, for example, 5 millivolts at 100 microamperes. Care should be taken to couple the three diodes thermally so that temperature differences among them are minimized.

If the reference input is made variable, as indicated by the dotted lines in Figure 12.1, a somewhat exotic characteristic results which is indicated analytically and graphically. It is shown for its general interest and possible utility in some special application.

The same idea of operating diodes at varying but always matching currents leads to the Selector Circuit of Figure 12.2. A glance back at Figure 6.21 will review the notion of voltage selection.

There are several reasons why potentiometers and operational amplifiers should work well together, and one controlling reason why they have not. It can be seen in Figure 2.4 that the gains of the various inputs to a weighted addition circuit depend not on the resistance through which they are introduced, but on its reciprocal; if the otherwise admirable potentiometer were a variable *conductance*, all would be well. Since it is not and since a device exhibiting this property in proportion to the turn of a dial is not in prospect, a basic problem exists in the design and in the utilization of operational circuits, particularly general-purpose analog computing structures. The next several circuits address

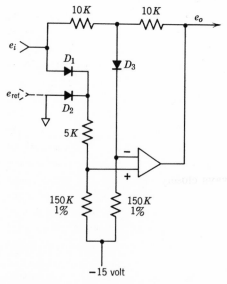

$$e_o = +|e_i|$$

Note: reverse diodes and bias voltage for $e_o = -|e_i|$

Figure 12.1.   Single-amplifier absolute value circuit.

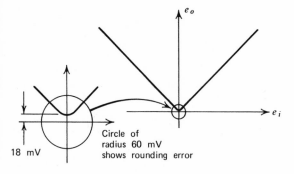

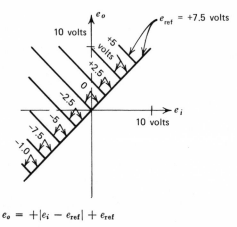

$$e_o = +|e_i - e_{ref}| + e_{ref}$$

Effect of variable reference voltage

Figure 12.1. (*Continued*).

this problem with the end in view of adapting the circuitry to the very highly developed conventional precision potentiometer, with its calibrated turns-counting dials and other refinements. *An important reservation:* potentiometers of whatever variety are to be treated with suspicion when any sort of fast circuitry is being considered. In the nature of things they are prey to all sorts of distributed parasitic effects. As a general rule, below 100 hertz they are fine, but above this frequency vigilance should rise proportionally.

The principal reason why analog computers have not had wide acceptance is the lack of an adequately dramatic output or display device of modest cost. This observation is consonant with the current interest in electronic music synthesizers, which are nothing more than analog computers with acoustic outputs. The next circuit has relevance to such synthesizers as well as to other situations where signals are to be accurately but conveniently combined in continuously variable proportions.

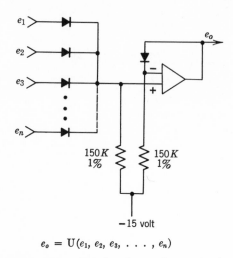

$$e_o = U(e_1, e_2, e_3, \ldots, e_n)$$

Figure 12.2.   Simple voltage-selector circuit.

The circuit in Figure 12.3 employs a voltage divider in its general form, an assertion that becomes more palatable when the e_2 input is imagined to be grounded, thus reducing the circuit to its more familiar form. The mixing ratio is linear with potentiometer setting, and the sum of the gains for the two inputs is precisely unity. The latter property entitles the circuit to be called a two-input weighted average computer. A multiple-input weighted averaging circuit works along the same lines,

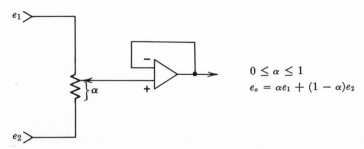

$$0 \leq \alpha \leq 1$$
$$e_o = \alpha e_1 + (1 - \alpha)e_2$$

Figure 12.3.   Linear additive mixing circuit.

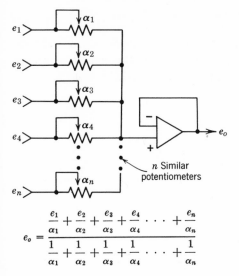

$$e_o = \frac{\dfrac{e_1}{\alpha_1} + \dfrac{e_2}{\alpha_2} + \dfrac{e_3}{\alpha_3} + \dfrac{e_4}{\alpha_4} \cdots + \dfrac{e_n}{\alpha_n}}{\dfrac{1}{\alpha_1} + \dfrac{1}{\alpha_2} + \dfrac{1}{\alpha_3} + \dfrac{1}{\alpha_4} \cdots + \dfrac{1}{\alpha_n}}$$

Figure 12.4. Multiple-input weighted average circuit.

but the potentiometer settings lose their simple interpretation. See Figure 12.4. If the effects of individual potentiometer settings are to retain their significance for a human operator in control of a weighted averaging process, a tree structure of two-input circuits is a workable though cumbersome approach to a problem that calls for a digital solution. See Figure 12.5. The linear combination of various contaminant concentra-

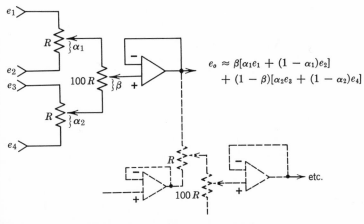

$$e_o \approx \beta[\alpha_1 e_1 + (1 - \alpha_1)e_2] + (1 - \beta)[\alpha_2 e_3 + (1 - \alpha_2)e_4]$$

Figure 12.5. Multiple-input weighted average circuit.

tions into a pollution index is one use that has been suggested for this sort of hardware.

The circuit of Figure 12.6 applies the principle of Figure 4.11 to enable the numerator and denominator of a fraction to be entered separately, perhaps a useful feature in equipment used by unskilled people.

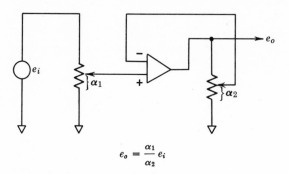

$$e_o = \frac{\alpha_1}{\alpha_2} e_i$$

Figure 12.6.   Numerator-denominator coefficient circuit.

The problem of setting coefficients in the general case has two parts, which are set forth below. The more familiar part of the problem is dispatched neatly by a circuit published by the Philbrick/Nexus organization. See Figure 12.7. The potentiometer setting is defined in terms of γ, which is zero when the wiper is centered and which equals ± 1 at the extremes. When $\gamma = -1$ the direct input is connected to ground and the

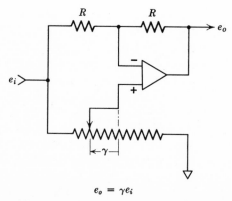

$$e_o = \gamma e_i$$

Figure 12.7.   Bipolar potentiometer circuit.

circuit functions as a simple invertor. When γ equals $+1$ the direct input is connected to the input signal and follower action at unity gain takes place. When the wiper is centered the circuit is a difference amplifier with its inputs tied together, which gives zero gain. At intermediate settings the gain is proportional to γ. Hence a wide range of bipolar coefficients may be set and read from a single dial.

The output of the potentiometer circuit above may be connected to the summing points of several computing amplifiers through appropriate fixed resistors. It may then be thought of as a coefficient circuit having multiple outputs, as represented in block form in Figure 12.8a. The

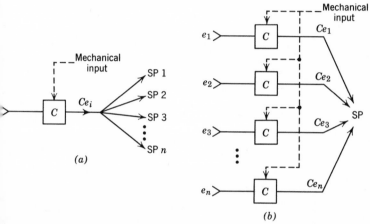

Figure 12.8. Adjustable coefficient circuit types. (a) Multiple output and (b) multiple input.

other important practical case is that in which a single coefficient must apply identically to several input signals to a summing point, which to judge from the block diagram in Figure 12.8b is something of a trick. It is done by converting the voltage signals into currents, which are summed by confluence at the wiper of a single potentiometer serving as a current divider. See Figure 12.9. The blocks labeled G are voltage-to-current converter circuits; each of these circuits, which may also be called voltage-controlled current sources, will be shown to involve an amplifier and four precision resistors. The amplifier with summing point labeled S' in the figure is a current invertor; it makes possible bipolar coefficients and also provides current compensation for the main amplifier. Signals connected to S' through fixed resistors appear uninverted at the output. If the feedback element Z_f is a capacitor the operation performed becomes integration of the sum of the inputs with respect to time, as introduced in Chapter 3. This scheme is intended for use with microcircuit amplifiers, preferably with the main and auxiliary amplifiers in the same package.

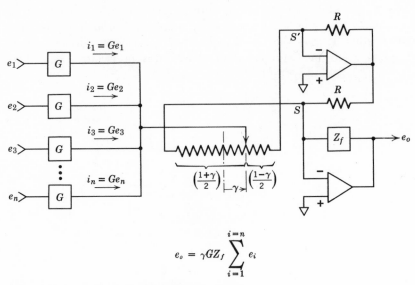

$$e_o = \gamma G Z_f \sum_{i=1}^{i=n} e_i$$

Figure 12.9. Current-divider coefficient circuit.

The operation of a potentiometer as a current divider requires explanation. The special case in which one side of the potentiometer is grounded for the voltage and current dividers is given in Figure 12.10. The voltage divider requires a high-resistance readout and is shown with a voltage follower; the current divider needs a virtual ground and thus is shown

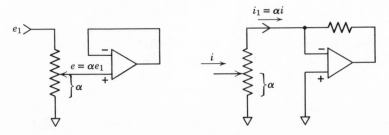

Figure 12.10. Voltage and current dividers.

with a current follower. The general case appears in Figure 12.11. Note that the current divider with two outputs and one input is just the reverse of the voltage divider. The striking similarity in the algebra is due to what is called duality in circuit theory. The algebra for the current divider works out neatly if expressed in terms·of the variable γ, defined in Figure 12.9.

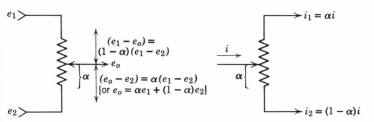

Figure 12.11.   General case of voltage and current dividers.

Both kinds of coefficient circuit have their place in computation machinery, ideally as dictated by the nature of the equations. It can be argued that both types be included in a general-purpose analog machine, although the questions of how many of which or how to switch from one to the other are problems familiar to those who have thought deeply about how to organize such an instrument. Figure 12.12 begs these questions in the grand manner by providing an indeterminate number of each. Even so, this diagram represents what is today a perfectly practical subunit of a general-purpose analog machine, and one which is not, thanks to microcircuit economics, prohibitively expensive. Note that the potentiometers may be set by digital voltmeter or other means without the possibility of loading error, although the attraction of dial setting and reading is considerable for small- or low-cost systems which may not include a digital meter.

An examination is necessary for the voltage-to-current converter circuit which was included in Figure 12.12; it is isolated in Figure 12.13. This remarkable circuit is attributed to the Lincoln Laboratory of M.I.T. and is called the Howland circuit after the inventor, Mr. Bradford Howland. Analytical treatments of circuits are usually unsatisfactory by reason of their complexity. In this case the reverse is true; the algebra drops out almost immediately, yielding the correct result but very little insight into how the circuit works. The graphical solution is more informative. The feedback network dictates that the output voltage be just twice the load voltage (see the V-R graph in the figure) ; the load current

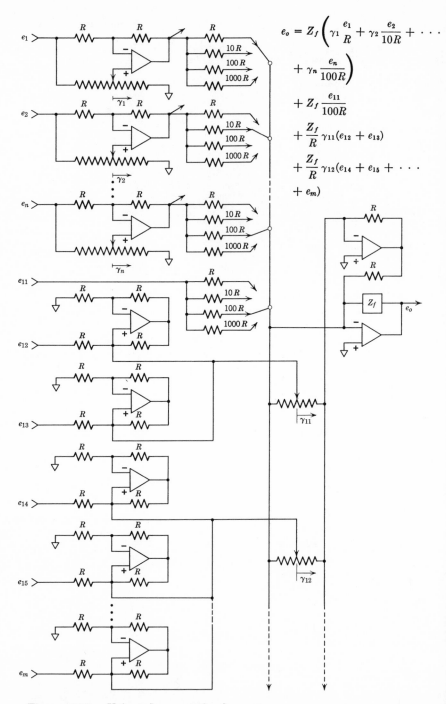

$$e_o = Z_f \left(\gamma_1 \frac{e_1}{R} + \gamma_2 \frac{e_2}{10R} + \cdots \right.$$

$$\left. + \gamma_n \frac{e_n}{100R} \right)$$

$$+ Z_f \frac{e_{11}}{100R}$$

$$+ \frac{Z_f}{R} \gamma_{11}(e_{12} + e_{13})$$

$$+ \frac{Z_f}{R} \gamma_{12}(e_{14} + e_{15} + \cdots$$

$$+ e_m)$$

Figure 12.12.   Universal computational operator.

156

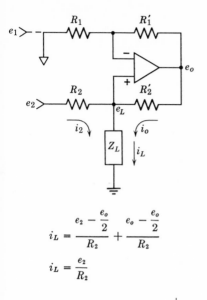

$$i_L = \frac{e_2 - \dfrac{e_o}{2}}{R_2} + \frac{e_o - \dfrac{e_o}{2}}{R_2}$$

$$i_L = \frac{e_2}{R_2}$$

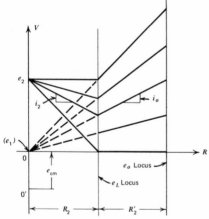

Figure 12.13. The Howland circuit—a voltage-to-current converter.

is the sum of i_2 from the input source, and i_o from the output terminal; the voltage-resistance graph shows these two currents (slopes) for various values of the load voltage. It is evident that their sum is constant. Note that the amplifier causes the resistor R'_2 to behave as a negative resistance, in that the higher the voltage the greater the current flow *out* of the terminal. This ability of the differential operational amplifier to cause a terminal to behave as if a negative impedance were connected

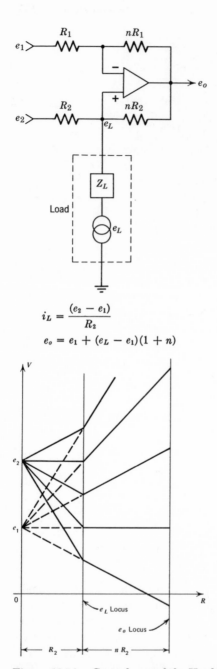

$$i_L = \frac{(e_2 - e_1)}{R_2}$$

$$e_o = e_1 + (e_L - e_1)(1 + n)$$

Figure 12.14. General case of the Howland circuit.

to it has many uses; the direct cancellation of an unwanted impedance (or admittance) is the most obvious, and at the same time the most startling.

The above presentation does not do full justice to the Howland circuit, which is in general a circuit with differential inputs. This property is most easily seen by noting that adding a voltage e_{cm} to both inputs corresponds with shifting the origin of the V-R graph to O', which leaves the slopes and thus the currents unaffected. Another important property of the circuit is that the output is proportional to the load voltage when the e_1 input is inactive (grounded). Note that the primed resistors may be a given multiple of their counterparts. The relation between the load voltage and the output voltage is that of a conventional follower-with-gain, and care should be taken that the output is not driven off scale. This last is the more important because both active and reactive loads are fair game for this circuit. The general case appears in Figure 12.14. Notice how the circuit responds to the extremes of load voltage shown; it is merely a linear system, but a most appealing one.

Figure 12.15 demonstrates by means of a block diagram and operator algebra that a first-order lag positively fed back at unity gain becomes a pure time integrator. The significance of this appears with the realization that the circuit of Figure 12.16 suffices to embody the block diagram.

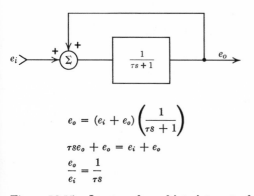

$$e_o = (e_i + e_o)\left(\frac{1}{\tau s + 1}\right)$$

$$\tau s e_o + e_o = e_i + e_o$$

$$\frac{e_o}{e_i} = \frac{1}{\tau s}$$

Figure 12.15.   Lag transformed into integrator by positive feedback.

The result is a noninverting integrator that can be readily and *rapidly* reset to zero or any other initial condition voltage by the closure of a simple switch (perhaps electronic) to a simple voltage source, and which is inherently balanced for input current integration errors. It can be made to serve as a summing integrator by splitting the input resistor

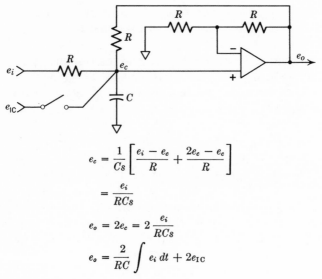

$$e_c = \frac{1}{Cs}\left[\frac{e_i - e_c}{R} + \frac{2e_c - e_c}{R}\right]$$

$$= \frac{e_i}{RCs}$$

$$e_o = 2e_c = 2\frac{e_i}{RCs}$$

$$e_o = \frac{2}{RC}\int e_i \, dt + 2e_{IC}$$

Figure 12.16.   Bootstrap integrator (noninverting).

into parallel branches having equivalent resistance, but usually such chores are assigned to a preceding summing amplifier. Although the circuit was arrived at by the route given above, it is interesting if somewhat deflating to recognize it as merely a Howland current-source circuit driving and simultaneously reading out the terminal voltage of a grounded capacitor. It is redrawn as such in Figure 12.17.

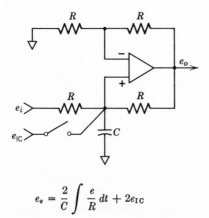

$$e_o = \frac{2}{C}\int \frac{e}{R} \, dt + 2e_{IC}$$

Figure 12.17.   Bootstrap integrator as an application of Howland circuit.

A voltage-controlled sawtooth wave generator is given in Figure 12.18; it is intended to illustrate the reset properties of the bootstrap integrator. No claim is made for the reset circuit except that it works up to a repetition rate of a few kilohertz. The slope of the ramp generated and hence the repetition rate of the sawtooth is proportional to the reference voltage, which may be a useful feature in a finished circuit design using this as a starting point.

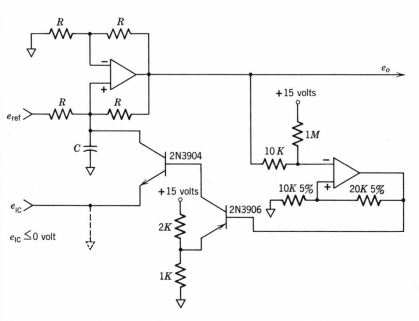

Figure 12.18. Voltage-controlled sawtooth generator.

A very elegant application of the bootstrap integrator occurs in the sine-cosine computer in Figure 12.19. This circuit is a refinement of what is usually called a two-phase oscillator. It computes the indicated functions of time, beginning at the instant the switch is opened; the amplitude invariance is provided by adjusting the damping control for constant amplitude over many cycles of computation. Unlike a conventional oscillator there is no nonlinear feedback to control the amplitude and hence no trace of distortion from this source in either output. The harmonic purity of this circuit represents the best that operational gear has to offer; the largest distortion components are finite gain errors and common-mode error in the bootstrap amplifier. It is interesting to cross plot the outputs on an oscilloscope, or better still, on an X-Y plotter. The very active field of digital-computer-controlled displays uses analog character-generation hardware of this sort—somewhat ironically because it is the only way to achieve the required information rates.

The availability of precise and precisely related sine and cosine voltages at frequencies from zero to well beyond the audio range leads directly to schemes for adjustable phase generators. Simply adding a small

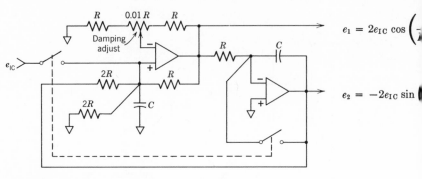

$$e_1 = 2e_{IC} \cos \left(\right.$$

$$e_2 = -2e_{IC} \sin$$

Figure 12.19. Sine- and cosine-wave generator.

variable fraction of one output of Figure 12.19 to the other provides a resultant of adjustable phase and approximately constant amplitude for phase shifts on the order of a few degrees. See Figure 12.20 in which the diagram discloses the vectorial significance of a simple addition of these inputs.

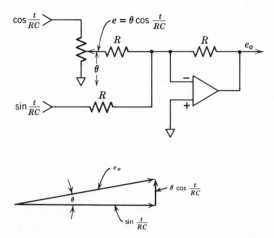

Figure 12.20. Principle of adjustable phase shifter.

The additive mixer circuit given earlier in this chapter serves as a phase-shift device enabling the phase of its output to be adjusted on both sides of the 45° line between the input phasors, while preserving approximately constant amplitude. See Figure 12.21. The relation between the potentiometer setting and the phase angle is precise although

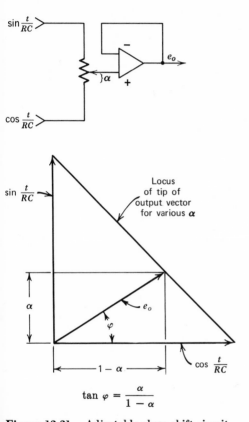

Figure 12.21. Adjustable phase-shift circuit.

nonlinear. Observe that all four quadrants are available by simply inverting one or both of the input signals. A strong desire to do something about the amplitude variation results from the contemplation of this circuit.

Given a ganged potentiometer and the above keen desire, a very appealing approximate circuit has been contrived. See Figure 12.22. When the potentiometer wiper is centered the gain of the follower-with-gain

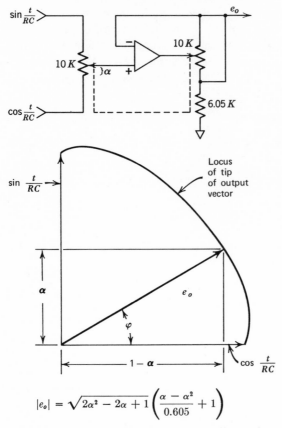

$$|e_o| = \sqrt{2\alpha^2 - 2\alpha + 1}\left(\frac{\alpha - \alpha^2}{0.605} + 1\right)$$

Figure 12.22.   Approximate constant-amplitude phase-shift circuit.

is $\sqrt{2}$; it is unity at the extremes. The amplitude variation is about 4% at the worst point, being governed by the expression given in the figure. The relation between phase angle and potentiometer setting is the same as before. This circuit appears germane to experimental work in a number of disciplines, especially because the approximate relationships it employs are precise and thus amenable to being "computed out" in the data-reduction phase of the work.

Note in the circuits above that the phase angle is quite independent of frequency.

It frequently happens that an otherwise attractive computation or instrumentation procedure does not yield the desired quantity, but instead its reciprocal. A circuit to correct this problem by computing the reciprocal of the input appears in Figure 12.23. It serves also to introduce

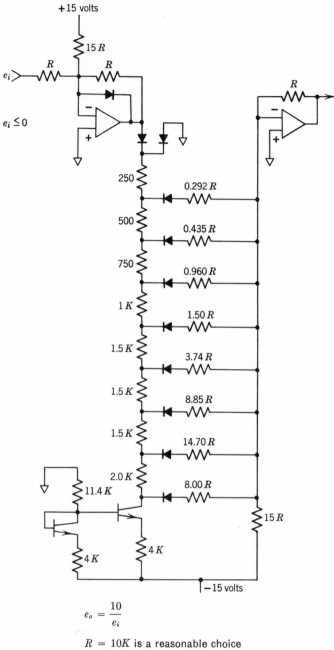

$$e_o = \frac{10}{e_i}$$

$R = 10K$ is a reasonable choice

    NPN: 2N 3904

    Diodes: 1N 914

Figure 12.23. Reciprocal computer using diode-function generator.

a powerful operational technique, the diode-function generator. This particular circuit is unconventional in that the function it embodies is monotonically decreasing, and because all of its diodes are conducting for zero input signal. Nevertheless the operating principle should be discernible. When the input signal is <1 volt the input amplifier is zero-bounded by its feedback diode, and the output is at +10 volts. See Figure 12.24.

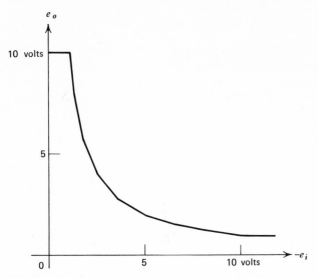

Figure 12.24.   Input-output characteristic of reciprocal computer.

As the input signal increases beyond 1 volt the output of the first amplifier moves positive and the output falls until at 1.25-volts input the uppermost diode ceases to conduct, causing what is called the first break point in the output function. Thereafter the diodes are switched off one by one, causing the series of slope discontinuities that enable the output to approximate the desired hyperbola. The slopes associated with each break point are set by the resistors in series with the diodes remaining in conduction. Finally at 10-volts input the last diode expires and the output remains at +1 volt, as set by the fixed bias resistor of value $15R$. There is an overall inversion in the circuit which has been omitted in this exposition; the circuit as drawn is appropriate for negative input signals, and the inversion is accounted for by plotting the negative of the input as the abscissa. The transistor circuit at the lower left of the diagram is a constant current source that causes the series string of low-value resistors to behave as a voltage source connected to the amplifier output and having many taps. The grounded diode near the output of the first amplifier handles the function generator when the amplifier is bounded, and is automatically switched out when the amplifier becomes active.

The frequency of the sine-cosine computer of Figure 12.19 is not readily changed, which is not a weakness but does call attention to the convenience of an adjustable sine-wave source. The next circuit is the first step in the development of the ultimate in adjustable generators. When used in conjunction with voltage-controlled triangular-wave generators developed in the systems chapter, it enables the construction of sinusoid generators in which the frequency is controlled linearly by an input voltage over a wide range. Furthermore, sine-cosine versions analogous to Figure 12.19 are perfectly straightforward, enabling the phase-shift trickery above to be applied.

The circuit in Figure 12.25 is in no sense an oscillator. It generates an output voltage that is the sine of the instantaneous input voltage, and is perhaps best thought of as a shaping circuit. The two-amplifier circuit on the left is a variation of the circuit of Figure 6.13; its function is to convert the input into $1\frac{1}{2}$ cycles of a triangular-wave function, approximating the final sinusoid. That is, it accounts for the large-scale periodicity of the sine function over a limited range of argument that is sufficient for a great many computation and simulation purposes.

The formidable circuit on the right is a diode function generator that is placed in the feedback path to progressively reduce the gain of the operational circuit, and thus carve down the triangular function into a sinusoid. That is, the whole feedback structure could be replaced by a "sine-shaped" nonlinear resistor. The diode function generator consists in part of a series string of low-value resistors that is connected at its center to the amplifier output and driven by transistor constant current sources at its ends. It thus serves as plus and minus voltage sources referenced to the output and having many taps. To each tap is connected a diode that is directed so as to block when the output voltage is zero. When the output swings, for example, negative, the upper diodes begin to conduct one by one, starting with the lowest. The resistors in series with the diodes are chosen to approximate the sine function with a series of straight line segments, which may be thought of as tangents or secants of the ideal function. The values given for these resistors are nominal; if used as given a functional accuracy of about 2% will result, provided matched diodes are used. This accuracy in most cases will suffice for the signal-generator applications of this shaping circuit.

Trigonometric computing applications require that the resistors be

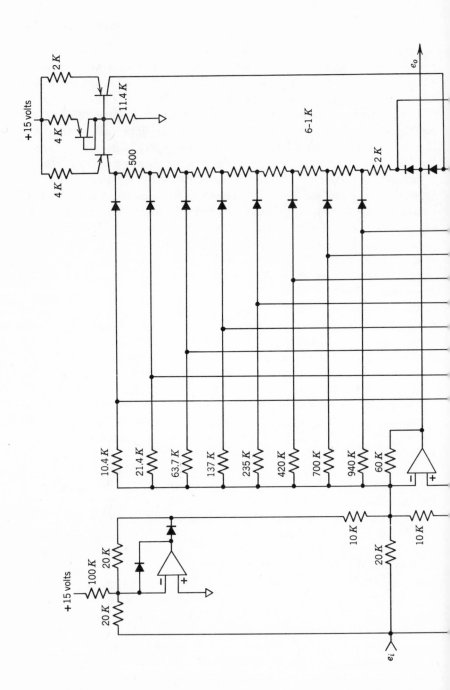

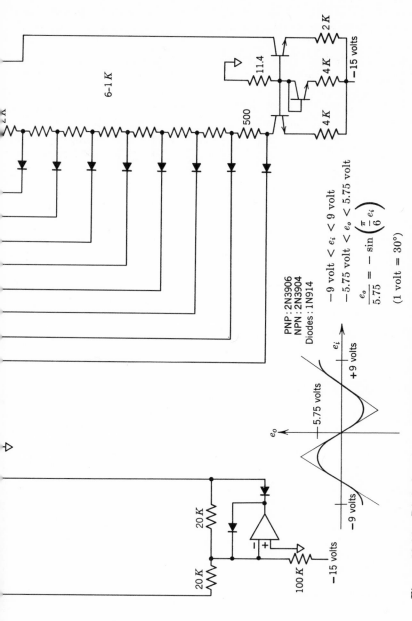

Figure 12.25. Diode-function generator for the sine of an input voltage.

-9 volt $< e_i < 9$ volt

-5.75 volt $< e_o < 5.75$ volt

$$\frac{e_o}{5.75} = -\sin\left(\frac{\pi}{6} e_i\right)$$

$(1 \text{ volt} = 30°)$

PNP : 2N3906
NPN : 2N3904
Diodes : 1N914

made adjustable and be carefully trimmed to conform to the sine function. If this is done the circuit is capable of accuracy better than 0.1% over several tens of degrees centigrade. Networks of this sort are available commercially and are unquestionably a bargain; thus for computing purposes the function-generator portion of this circuit is purely illustrative. There are situations where some trigonometric-operator action is better than none, and in these cases this circuit may be worth constructing. The sharing of the gain-setting resistors by signals of both polarities helps to ensure that the generated function is at least symmetric about the zero axis. The transfer characteristic of the function generator appears in Figure 12.26 along with the ideal (smooth) function displaced vertically; the segmentation is imperceptible. The gradual conduction characteristic of the diodes (the same phenomenon that produces the

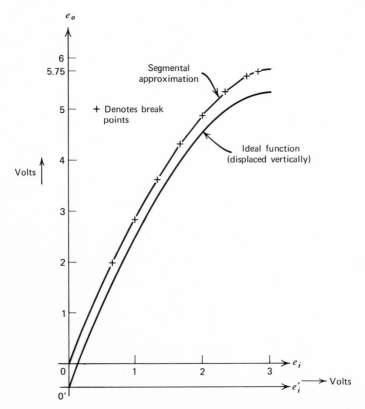

Figure 12.26. Input-out characteristic of sine-function generator. (All quadrants typical.)

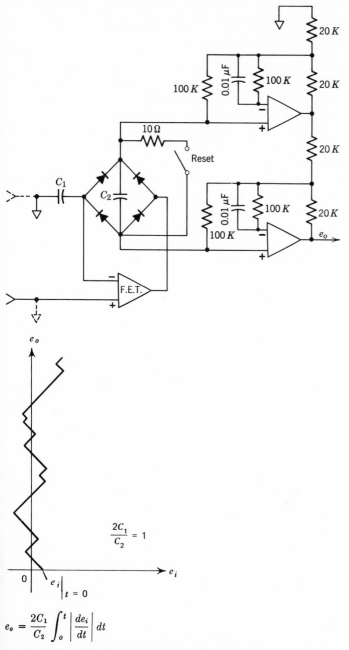

Figure 12.27. Signal-variation accumulator circuit.

$$e_o = \frac{2C_1}{C_2} \int_o^t \left| \frac{de_i}{dt} \right| dt$$

rounding error at the origin in the absolute-value circuit of Figure 12.1) reduces the segmentation in the actual output below that of the theoretical segmental approximation, illustrating that nature is not invariably recalcitrant.

The circuit of Figure 12.27 is unusual and useful, but difficult to name. After the reset switch has been momentarily closed the input-output relationship is as shown, the output monotonically increasing in response to increments *and* decrements of the input. If the input signal represents the position along a line of an experimental animal or the market value of a security, then the output is a measure of the *activity* following the last reset. The equation in the figure states the performance exactly, but the operations it denotes are largely implicit in the actual circuit. The diode bridge causes the currents for charging and discharging C_1 in response to input variations to cumulatively charge C_2; the voltage across C_2 is read out by the differential follower. Noise on the input causes the output to appear to drift, whereas in fact it is responding as intended to the noise as signal. The possibility of using this circuit to quantify noise has not been examined. Input currents cause direct errors, and F.E.T. amplifiers are recommended for this reason, although the difference amplifier with the current compensation resistors shown gives fair performance with conventional transistor amplifiers. The 10-ohm resistor in series with the reset switch limits the discharge current; the capacitors should be polystyrene. The dotted lines indicate that a single-ended amplifier can be used if, for example, chopper-stabilization is desired. In this case the signal source must be able to drive the capacitive load—namely, C_1 to ground.

A noteworthy application of the circuit above is a staircase waveform generator, which it becomes when driven by a square wave. The reset switch must be synchronized with the square wave if the timing of the staircase is important. A gated multivibrator given in the next chapter neatly obviates this timing requirement.

The relative difficulty of devising precise limiter or clipper circuits was remarked in Chapter 6. The next circuit is such a limiter that in addition is voltage controlled. See Figure 12.28. The circuit is a concatenation of biased zero-bound circuits of the type shown in Figure 6.8, followed by a summing amplifier to restore the zero level of the output. The graphical proof given also demonstrates the near necessity of a geometrical approach to problems of this kind. The amplifiers are single-ended, which adapts the circuit to chopper stabilization and to implementation on general-purpose machines. A word of warning: the availability of this circuit may lead initially to a faulty simulation

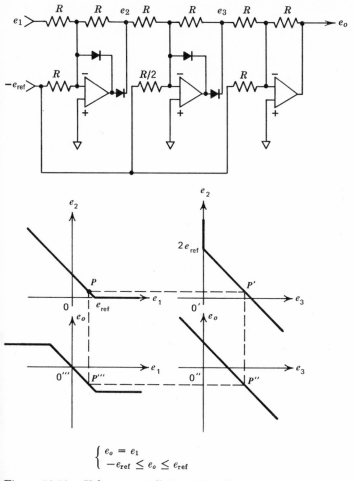

Figure 12.28. Voltage-controlled precision limiter.

of a mechanical or optical system. An attractive circuit does not repeal the physical laws on which correct simulation depends.

The need occasionally arises for a precise hysteresis circuit. Henry Paynter has shown how hysteresis follows from the application of positive feedback to a limiter. This principle is applied to construct a precise, voltage-controlled hysteresis circuit based on the limiter above. This may be done either by adding an inverting amplifier to the structure of Figure 12.28, or by altering that structure by making the final ampli-

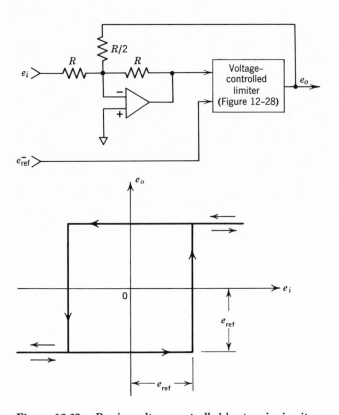

Figure 12.29. Precise voltage-controlled hysteresis circuit.

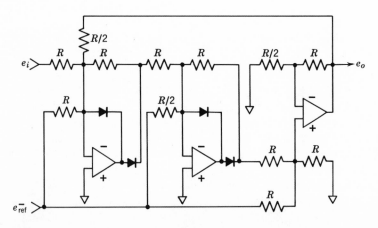

Figure 12.30. Precise voltage-controlled hysteresis circuit.

174

fier into an adder-subtractor. These alternatives are presented in Figures 12.29 and 12.30, the input-output characteristics of which are identical. The resulting hysteresis loop is square, which simplifies the somewhat tricky task of scaling apparatus of this kind.

The reference voltage in all three circuits above must be negative. If it is desired to use a positive voltage as the reference, simply reverse all diodes.

Chapter XIII

Switching Circuits

Except for the two hysteresis circuits discussed in the preceding chapter, all the circuitry up to this point has dealt with continuous signals in continuous fashion—the nearest thing to a discontinuity being one of slope, as at the break point of a diode circuit. Operational circuits involving switching and discrete-value signals exist in three categories: (1) event detectors treat continuous operational input signals and yield discrete output levels denoting that the event has or has not occurred; level-crossing detectors are an example. (2) Operational switches change the mode of an operational circuit or the destination of a signal in response to discrete control signals; track and hold circuits are an important case in point. (3) Pure switching circuits perform the "clockwork" functions ancillary to automatic operational systems. These functions are implemented with operational amplifiers purely for convenience, both practical and even more important, conceptual.

A signal crossing a reference or threshold level is the simplest event, but the implications of the accurate and prompt detection of it are profound. Figure 13.1 presents the simplest detector for a voltage-crossing event—merely a differential operational amplifier. It is accurate but slow. The amplifier is in saturation except when switching, and depending on the amplifier type, it may take as long as several milliseconds to recover from saturation. Although amplifiers are available that recover in well under 1 millisecond, it should be clear that the approach to electronic speed lies in other directions.

The basic crossing-detector configuration is shown in Figure 13.2; it

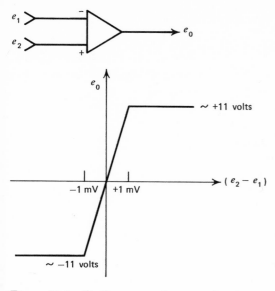

Figure 13.1. Rudimentary voltage-crossing detector.

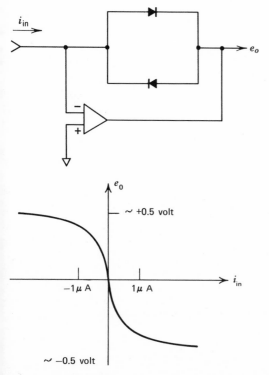

Figure 13.2. Principle of current-crossing detector.

is a current follower with feedback bounds—diodes in the simplest case. Depending on the direction of the input current, the amplifier is bounded by one diode or the other, and thus is always operating linearly and preserving the voltage null and current balance at its summing point. A shift of a fraction of a microampere sends the output flying to the other bound, where feedback through the oppositely directed diode maintains the equilibrium. The performance of this current direction detector is much improved, especially at low currents, by the added components shown in Figure 13.3. The current in the first diode is identically the

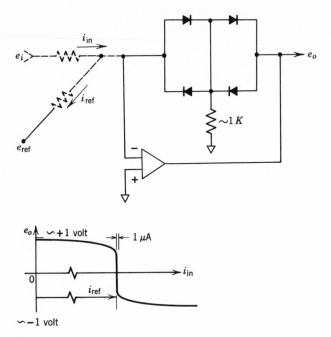

Figure 13.3.   Current-biased current-crossing detector.

input-signal current, and when this is on the order of a microampere there are only about 400 millivolts across the diode, which behaves like the logarithmic resistor that it really is, and very little like the ideal diode desired. The $1K$ resistor insures that there will be 400 microamperes flowing in the second diode, which behaves very crisply indeed. In addition, any leakage current through the second diode flows harmlessly to ground through the resistor and does not reach the summing point, a consideration that is sometimes important (for example, in the rate-detector circuit of the next paragraph). The current detector becomes a fast voltage-crossing detector when equipped with a pair of resistors, one for the signal and the other for the reference voltage, as shown by the dashed lines.

If the input element is a capacitor, the current detector responds to the rate of change of the input voltage, as shown in Figure 13.4. This

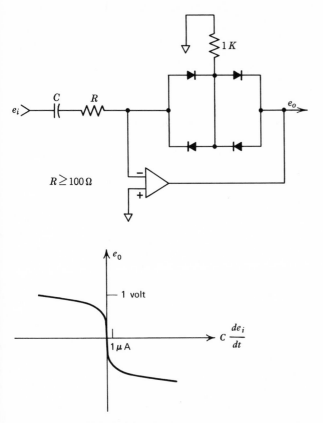

Figure 13.4. Rate-crossing detector (one-bit differentiator).

circuit is not as difficult to stabilize as a conventional linear differentiator; the resistor shown is usually sufficient. It is exactly as sensitive to input current error, however, and an F.E.T. amplifier is required to resolve slowly changing signals with a capacitor of reasonable size. A parametric amplifier would give really superb performance, and is not necessarily too high a price to pay for one bit of information, for the bit in question can be strategic. A change in the sign of the derivative accompanies a peak or valley of the signal (a local maximum or minimum); this circuit may thus be regarded as a peak-event detector;

it is so used in a peak-sensitive demodulation system in the next chapter.

The next circuit gives no output when the magnitude of the input signal is less than a reference voltage, yet gives a large output level when the input magnitude exceeds the reference. See Figure 13.5. It

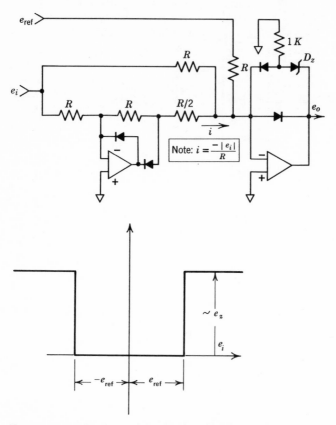

Figure 13.5. Precise symmetric magnitude detector.

is called a magnitude detector because its behavior is independent of the sign or polarity of the input. The circuit comprises an absolute value circuit followed by a biased crossing detector similar in principle to the one described above, but using a zener diode to give a large output swing in one direction. The no-output state is actually a fraction of a volt negative corresponding to the drop across the single bounding diode. The absolute value circuit is the classical precision circuit for this function. The first amplifier is a simple zero-bound circuit having zero gain for negative inputs and minus unity gain for positive input signals. Thus for positive input signals the invertor drives twice as much current to the second summing point as arrives by way of the upper resistor from the input proper. In this way the same net current is delivered regardless of the sign of the input signal, which is how the absolute value function is implemented. The algebraic sum of this absolute value current and the reference current is acted on by the current direction detector formed by the second amplifier. Note that the reference voltage must be positive. When the reference voltage is a "live" system variable this is the circuit of choice.

When the reference is a fixed constant a simpler circuit will serve for relatively slow signals. Note in Figure 13.6 that the detection levels

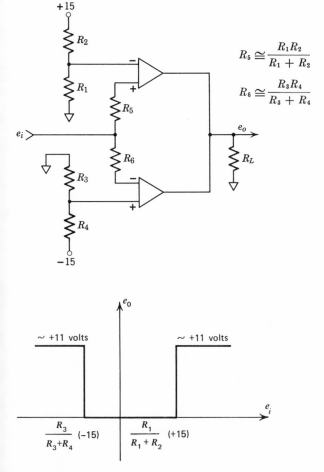

$$R_5 \cong \frac{R_1 R_2}{R_1 + R_2}$$

$$R_6 \cong \frac{R_3 R_4}{R_3 + R_4}$$

Figure 13.6. Precise magnitude detector.

can be made different for the two polarities—and that they will in fact be different unless the resistive dividers and the reference voltages match exactly—something of a mixed blessing. The same remarks apply to the nonsaturating and therefore quick version in Figure 13.7. Both circuits can be used with time varying references or used for the symmetric

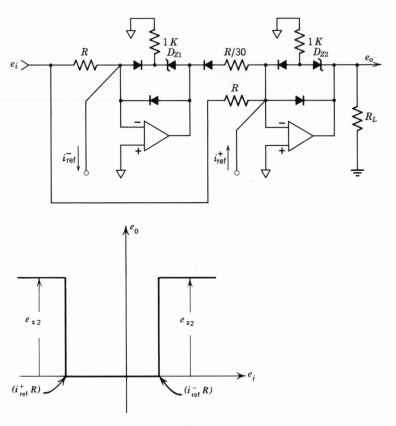

Figure 13.7. Fast-precision magnitude detector.

case if the reference and its negative are available. The fast version uses single-ended amplifiers with the usual corollaries as to chopper stabilization and computer use.

In Figure 13.7 negative signals act directly on the second amplifier, whereas positive signals initially cause the first amplifier to switch to its large output state (negative), which is then coupled through the diode and the small resistor to cause the second amplifier to switch by brute force.

When it is desired that the output reflect the sign of the input, the slightly modified circuits of Figures 13.8 and 13.9 serve, subject to the same remarks. Note that the absolute-value technique cannot be used.

In the preceding circuits the output was a switching variable as opposed to an operational variable, and thus the accuracy of its magnitude was not a concern. There are situations in which the output is significant in both ways, for example the hysteresis circuit, and for these an accu-

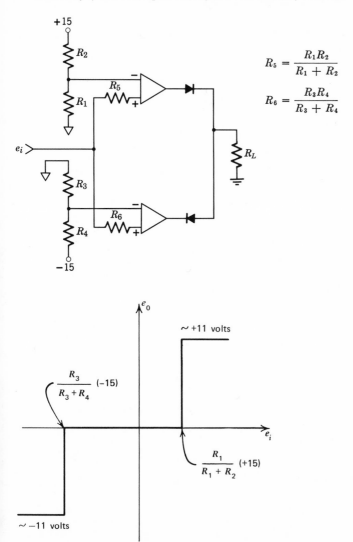

$$R_5 = \frac{R_1 R_2}{R_1 + R_2}$$

$$R_6 = \frac{R_3 R_4}{R_3 + R_4}$$

Figure 13.8. Precise dual-threshold detector.

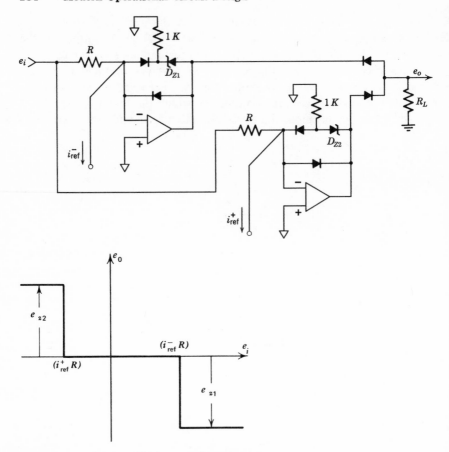

Figure 13.9.   Fast-precision dual-threshold detector.

rately bounded amplifier is required. Figure 13.10 illustrates how an accurate and accurately symmetric bound circuit is arranged. The scheme is to place a voltage reference source in a full-wave diode bridge as the feedback element. The voltage reference is shown as a battery and could actually be a mercury battery; a better reference is a zener diode operated at constant current. As shown in the figure a diode-connected transistor may substitute for the approximate 7-volt zener in ordinary applications. The base-emitter junction of the transistor zeners nicely when supplied with about 1 milliampere of bias current, which is the function served by the $15K$ resistors. When the input current is in the direction of the arrow the output swings negative until diodes D_1 and D_3 conduct, allowing the signal current to flow through them and the

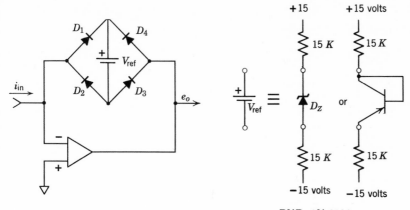

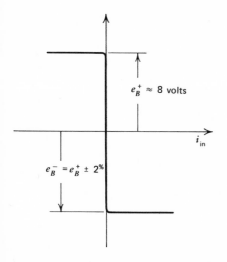

Figure 13.10. Inexpensive symmetric bounded amplifier.

reference source to the output. When the current reverses, diodes D_2 and D_4 conduct and the output is at its positive limit. It is faintly amusing to observe that if the reference is in fact a battery the direction of the signal current is such as to forever charge it; this incidentally explains why the shelf life is a reliable guide to the life of a battery in this kind of service.

Modern zener reference technology makes the mercury-cell reference an anachronism; it is this kind of reference diode that is intended in

Figure 13.11; its temperature coefficient should be such that when run at the recommended current it just cancels that of the two forward-biased junctions (representing the bridge diodes). It is reasonable to buy the diode bridge, or better still the whole thing as a specified package, from

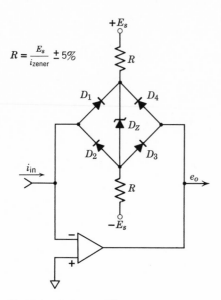

$$R = \frac{E_s}{i_{\text{zener}}} \pm 5\%$$

D_Z: 6.8 volt @ 1 milliampere

D_1, D_2: 1N 914 matched within 10 millivolt @ 1 microampere

D_3, D_4: 1N 914 matched within 10 millivolt @ 0.5 milliampere

$$e_o = \begin{cases} e_B^+ = +(V_{D_z} + V_{D_4} + V_{D_2}), & i_{\text{in}} < 0 \\ e_B^- = -(V_{D_z} + V_{D_3} + V_{D_1}), & i_{\text{in}} > 0 \end{cases}$$

Figure 13.11.   Moderate-precision bounded amplifier.

the maker of the reference diode, for really serious stability with temperature and time. In any event all diodes should be thermally coupled. The biasing resistors are chosen according to the formula in the figure.

The reason for this emphasis on accuracy is that, given an accurate reference, the hysteresis circuit of Figure 13.12 can approach the accuracy of the elaborate circuit given in the previous chapter (Figure 12.30). Its operating principle is the same, that is, positive feedback applied around an accurately limiting amplifier. The circuit switches state when the input current is just sufficient to overcome the current through the positive feedback resistor. If the input resistor is made equal to the feedback resistor, a square hysteresis loop results in terms of input and

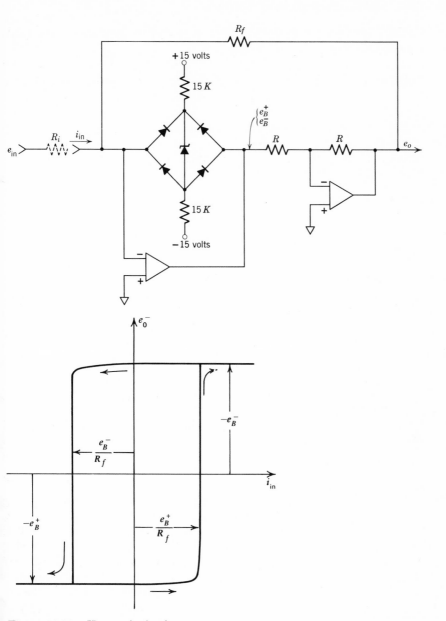

Figure 13.12. Hysteresis circuit.

output voltages. The convenience of a conventional operational summing point is considerable; the same basic idea will be exploited to construct a variety of pure switching circuits toward the end of this chapter.

Track and hold circuits are prominent in the category of operational circuits that modulate their mode of action in response to switched command signals. The design of these circuits relies on the field-effect transistor in the roles of analog switch and of high-resistance readout device for the holding capacitor. The nature of track and hold action is defined graphically in the time history of Figure 13.13. A simple track and

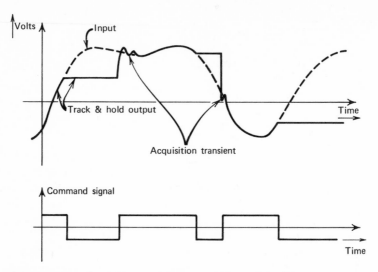

Figure 13.13. Time history defining track and hold action.

hold circuit that is serviceable for short (less than 1 second) holding periods will be found in Figure 13.14. The F.E.T. switches are driven in push-pull fashion, one on and the other off. In the track mode switch S_1 is on and the tracking loop comprises the input amplifier, S_1, the holding capacitor, the second amplifier as a current-compensated follower reading out the capacitor voltage, and feedback from the circuit output through the 20K resistor to the inverting input of the first amplifier (also configured as a voltage follower). The hold command causes S_1 to open; the voltage on the capacitor at the instant of the hold command ideally persists for the duration of the hold interval. The first amplifier is prevented from saturating by feedback through the conducting switch S_2. The 20K resistor prevents the two amplifiers, each a follower with an input signal of its own, from "fighting each other." When the track

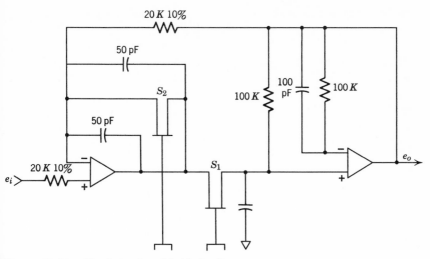

Figure 13.14.   Simple track and hold circuit.

command reappears there will be in general a large step input to the tracking loop, due to the tracking signal variation during the hold interval. The resulting nonlinear transient is identified as an acquisition transient; it calls attention to an inherent limitation: a track and hold circuit is not a *sampling* circuit of high performance. The specialty of the track and hold circuit is precise tracking, an accurate transition to the hold mode, and accurate holding. High-speed sampling is a different requirement and one to which feedback techniques are not well adapted.

An arrangement for demonstrating and testing track and hold circuits is given in Figure 13.15, because such a circuit in isolation has little to offer. The output of the voltage-crossing detector may be displayed on the second beam of a dual-beam oscilloscope, and the combined performance of the track and hold circuit and its associated logic-driver circuit may be inspected on the first beam. An important point resides here: those planning to use a track and hold circuit should think long and hard about how to verify its performance. Time synchrony is only one of the questions to be answered. Does the output really track accurately, and does it make the transition to hold mode without some sort of jump phenomenon to cause a systematic error? An X-Y plot of input versus output may help to answer these necessarily nasty questions.

A logic driver suitable for use with 15-volt power supplies is given in Figure 13.16. It works well even when casually constructed. In the

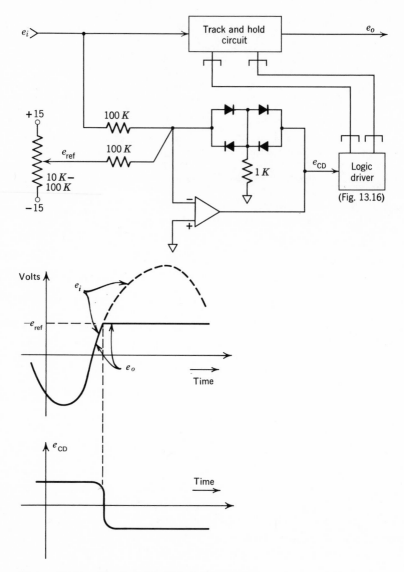

Figure 13.15. Track and hold test arrangement.

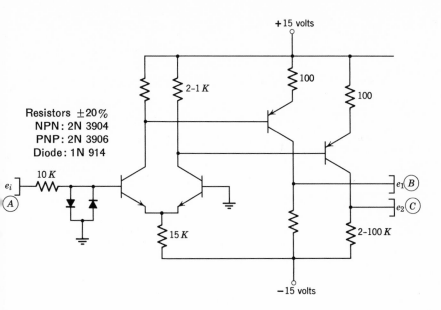

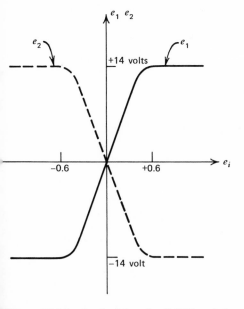

Figure 13.16. Logic driver for F.E.T. switch.

track and hold circuit itself care is required to minimize leakage from the capacitor, the more so as low error rates in hold mode are expected from the refined circuits below.

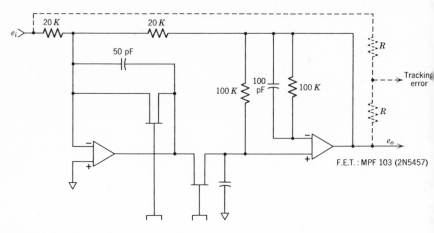

Figure 13.17.   Simple track and hold circuit (inverting).

Figure 13.17 illustrates that the input amplifier may just as easily be an invertor, if an overall inversion is desired. The same applies to the circuits below although it will not be illustrated. Note that tracking error may be examined critically in the inverting case by the simple means of looking at the midpoint of an accurate resistive divider connected between input and output, as shown dashed in the figure.

Figure 13.18 interposes the superb input resistance and low-input cur-

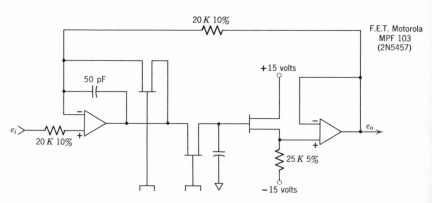

Figure 13.18.   Inexpensive track and hold circuit.

rent of an F.E.T. between the capacitor and the amplifier. The substantial voltage offset of the F.E.T. source-follower circuit is reduced to insignificance by the gain of the first operational amplifier ahead of it.

Figure 13.19 uses an F.E.T. operational amplifier because its freedom from macroscopic voltage offset enables the diode-resistor decoupling

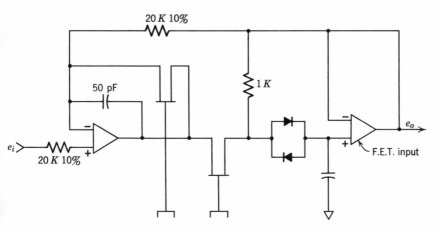

Figure 13.19. High-performance track and hold circuit.

circuit to be used to combat leakage at high temperature. The CMRR of the F.E.T. amplifier is not critical because of the gain ahead of it; the same is true of its voltage stability. This circuit offers superb performance over an extended temperature range.

The ability to control the routing of precise operational signals automatically at electronic speeds has enormous import. Two specimen circuits appear in Figures 13.20 and 13.21. The principal defect of the F.E.T. as an analog switch has been its on-resistance that ranges from perhaps 20 to 300 ohms. These circuits defeat that problem by the way the switch is deployed. The first circuit does so by placing the switch at the amplifier output with the operational loop closed around it. The second places the F.E.T. in series with the amplifier input terminal, a point known to be of very high impedance. These switches may be implemented with the logic driver of Figure 13.17. Switches that select from multiple paths may be arranged in the same fashion, provided that suitable logic precedes the driver circuit.

A basic bounded amplifier configuration is isolated in Figure 13.22, along with the input-output characteristic that qualifies it for a multi-

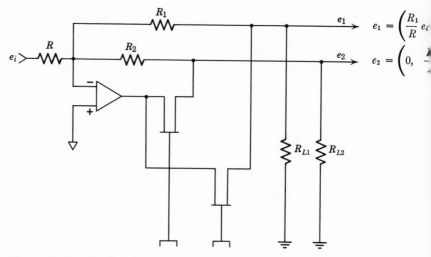

$$e_1 = \left(\frac{R_1}{R} e_i\right.$$

$$e_2 = \left(0,\right.$$

Figure 13.20. Single-pole double-output electronic switch.

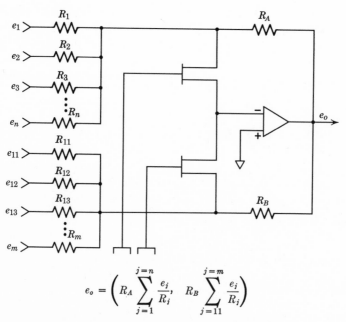

$$e_o = \left(R_A \sum_{j=1}^{j=n} \frac{e_j}{R_j}, \quad R_B \sum_{j=11}^{j=m} \frac{e_j}{R_j}\right)$$

Figure 13.21. Single-pole double-input electronic switch.

194

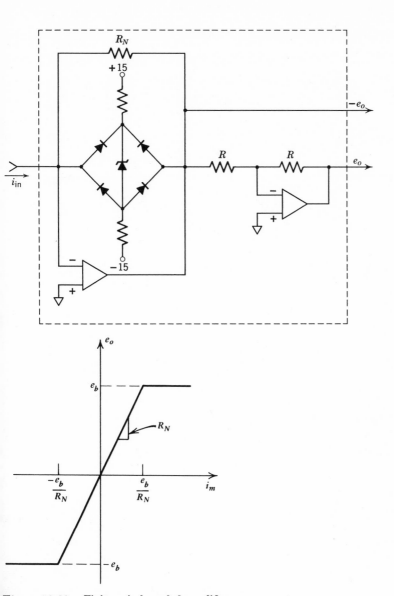

Figure 13.22. Finite-gain bounded amplifier.

plicity of switching circuit duties when used with rather simple feedback arrangements. A negative feedback resistor R_N has been placed around the bounded amplifier (of the type shown in Figure 13.10) in order to make its gain well-defined and to establish definite "corners" or "knees" in its characteristic, the significance of which will shortly be explained.

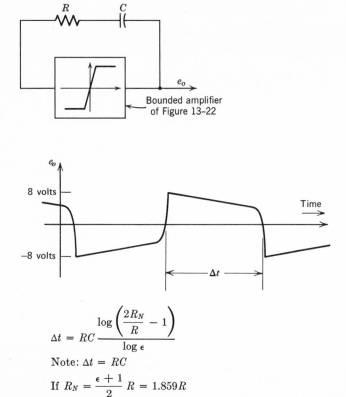

$$\Delta t = RC \frac{\log\left(\dfrac{2R_N}{R} - 1\right)}{\log \epsilon}$$

Note: $\Delta t = RC$

If $R_N = \dfrac{\epsilon + 1}{2} R = 1.859R$

Figure 13.23.   Freerunning multivibrator (square-wave generator).

Figure 13.23 shows how a square-wave generator is constructed using the basic circuit of Figure 13.22 and a series RC (positive) feedback network. The half-period is given with precision by the expression in the figure; the positive feedback resistor R must be smaller than the negative feedback resistor R_N to permit the regeneration on which multivibration depends. This form of multivibrator is called *astable,* and therein lies a clue to how it works. The circuit has no permanently stable state, but only two temporarily stable states and a reflexive transition from one to the other. The temporary stable states are those in which the amplifier is bounded. If, for purposes of explanation, the amplifier is assumed to relax from one of the bounded states past the corner of the characteristic into the central linear region, the output will tend toward zero under the influence of the negative feedback through R_N. Once it begins to move, however, there is a regenerative acceleration caused by the changing output voltage through C driving net positive feedback current through the smaller resistor R to the summing point, which causes the output to fly past the zero axis and literally slam into the other limit. This accelerative action can be observed by careful examination of the output waveform on an oscilloscope. It is exaggerated in the waveform drawn in Figure 13.23. The result of the sudden transition is to place an approximate 16-volt step of voltage on the RC feedback network; the result is a decaying exponential of current delivered to the summing point of such a sign as to keep the output jammed against the bound. When this current has decayed to the point where it just equals the opposite current through R_N, the reverse transition takes place, again with a vengeance.

The positive feedback is rate-dependent because of the capacitor, and it is conceivable that as long as the output does not change there will be zero regeneration and thus no action. But the situation is strictly analogous to a half-cone balanced on its vertex, and in practice either noise or a slight dissymmetry when the circuit is turned on are sufficient to make it go.

Further close attention to the oscilloscope will reveal that the output wave is not really square in its flat portion, but actually relaxes ever so slightly toward the zero axis with time. This feature is also shown exaggerated in Figure 13.23. What is happening is that the bounded amplifier relaxes along its bound line as the current from the RC network decays. The bound line has nonzero slope because the bound circuit has some resistance, and when the positive feedback current has decayed to such an extent that the knee of the characteristic in Figure 13.22 is passed, then switching occurs because the loop gain abruptly rises as the knee is passed. These minor discrepancies in the wave shape usually will not reduce the utility of the output, but if a very nearly perfect square wave is needed it can be made by following this circuit with another bounded amplifier, made by driving the circuit of Figure 13.10 through a resistor.

If a constant bias current is fed to the summing point of the square-wave generator of Figure 13.23, it will alter the symmetry of the wave by making the duration of the positive semiperiod different from that of the negative. When the bias current becomes equal to the current through the negative feedback resistor, the multivibration ceases and the circuit remains in one bounded state—it is said to be *monostable*. See Figure 13.24. The bias current, provided by a fixed resistor to the negative supply voltage, is such that the bounded amplifier operates

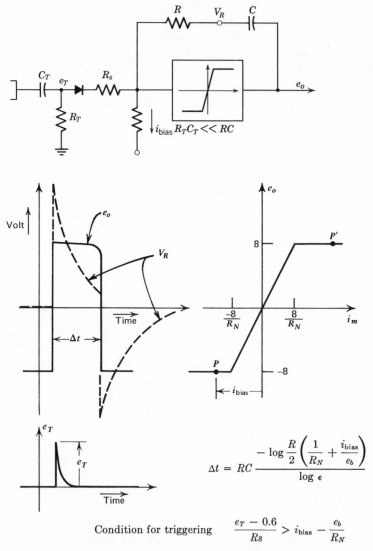

$$\Delta t = RC \, \frac{-\log \dfrac{R}{2}\left(\dfrac{1}{R_N} + \dfrac{i_{bias}}{e_b}\right)}{\log \epsilon}$$

Condition for triggering $\dfrac{e_T - 0.6}{Rs} > i_{bias} - \dfrac{e_b}{R_N}$

Figure 13.24.   Monostable multivibrator (one-shot).

at point P on its negative bound line. If by some means input current is supplied so as to move the operating point to the right, beyond the knee of the curve ever so slightly and for ever so short a period of time, then the circuit becomes regenerative and will execute one half-cycle of a multivibration before coming to rest once more at P. In other words, given that the circuit is operating instantaneously at a point to the right of the knee, inexorable causality requires that it vibrate once. The time spent in the quasistable state is given with precision by the expression in the figure. The usual means of changing the operating point is a short pulse of current called a trigger pulse. Either a pulse, or what is equivalent, a step transition applied to the trigger input, will do the job provided it is larger than the critical voltage e_T given by the inequation in the figure. The network composed of C_T and R_T converts a step transition into a pulse of equal height, while simply passing pulses unchanged. The circuit as drawn is triggered by positive pulses or positive-going transitions. Reversing the bias voltage and the diode makes the circuit respond to negative trigger events. The function of the diode is to block pulses of the wrong polarity. Note that the negative, or in switching circuit parlance, the complement of the output is available as the output of the first amplifier of the pair that make up the basic bounded amplifier.

The ultimate utility of this and related switching circuits depends on there being not a shred of doubt in the would-be user's mind about how they work. No hint of vagueness about the circuit mechanics should be tolerated, for to do so is to abdicate a whole realm rich in possibility, as the examples in the systems chapter are intended to illustrate.

Accordingly, another explanation of how the one-shot multivibrator works: the circuit is initially at rest at point P on the characteristic in Figure 13.24, operating there because of the bias current. Because the output is 8-volts negative, the right-hand plate of C is charged 8-volts negative with respect to the left-hand plate. A positive trigger pulse occurs, driving enough current through the diode and R_S to momentarily shift the operating point to the right of the knee. Once in the high-gain region the output makes an accelerating transition to some point P' on the other bound line because of positive feedback through C and R. Because the charge on C cannot change much in the extremely short time of the transition, the voltage at the junction of C and R, called V_R in the figure, is about $+16$ volts immediately after the transition. This voltage and thus the current through R decay exponentially with time constant RC; meanwhile, the operating point relaxes from P' toward the knee. The reverse transition occurs when the current through R minus the bias current just equals the knee current. The

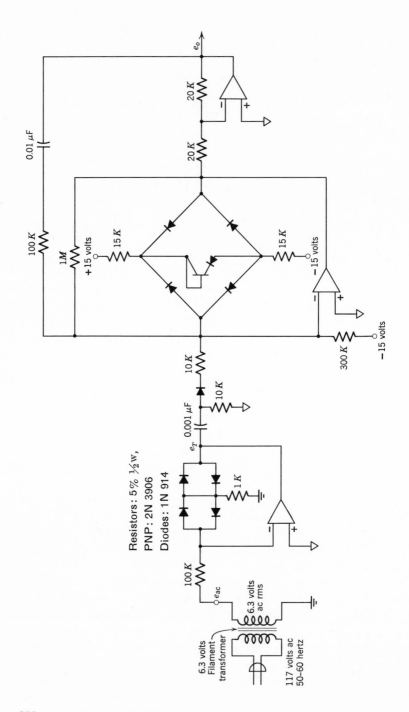

Resistors: 5% ½w,
PNP: 2N 3906
Diodes: 1N 914

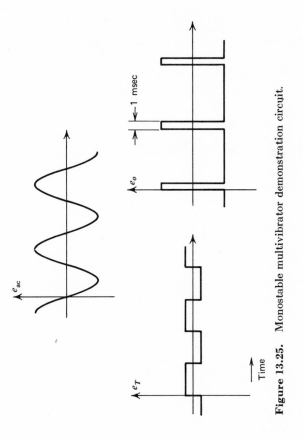

Figure 13.25. Monostable multivibrator demonstration circuit.

transition imposes a 16-volt negative step on the voltage V_R, due to coupling through the capacitor (as explained above). Thus V_R is substantially negative immediately after the return to the stable state; it decays to zero with time constant RC. When V_R has decayed to essentially zero the circuit is once more in its initial state, ready to be triggered again.

All the waveforms may be observed easily on an oscilloscope synchronized externally on the output signal. The next step in understanding the circuit is to connect it and observe it in action. To encourage the actual taking of this step, a test setup requiring a minimum of test equipment is given in Figure 13.25. A glance ahead to Chapter 15 is recommended for a description of operational amplifier hardware in its most convenient form. The first amplifier is a voltage zero-crossing detector based on Figure 13.3, which is used to convert the power line waveform into a square wave having coincident zero crossings. This square wave triggers the multivibrator on its positive transitions; the one-shot multivibrator puts out a positive pulse of 1-millisecond duration. With the circuit working and displaying the waveforms given in the figure, it is then advisable to play with it in various ways. For example, by reversing the bias voltage and the trigger diode. Adding a second 0.01-microfarad capacitor in parallel with the first will be seen to double the period. Note well: each such modification should be carefully undone, the circuit returned to its original state, and its performance verified before proceeding to the next. To ignore this rule is to invite confusion and loss of time. The design procedure used to arrive at this circuit is given in Figure 13.26 along with the actual circuit design as a numerical example.

If the capacitor C in Figure 13.25 is increased by a factor of 10 to 0.1 microfarad, it will be seen that the circuit misses every other positive transition of e_T. This is due to the voltage V_R not having sufficient time to decay to zero after the return to the stable state. There is thus a dormant interval after the recovery. In the first part of this dormant interval the circuit cannot be triggered, and in the latter part of it the circuit can be triggered but should not be, because the period will be incorrect due to the charge on C not having reached its equilibrium. The addition of the diode and resistor shown in Figure 13.27 may be seen experimentally to correct the situation, allowing proper triggering once again with the 10-millisecond period. As may be seen from the V_R waveform, the time constant after the reset has been made shorter by a factor of 10 without affecting the period. It is sometimes of practical importance to have a so-called zero-recovery one shot, and this is one approach.

Basic equation:

$$\Delta t = RC \, \frac{-\log \dfrac{R}{2}\left(\dfrac{1}{R_N} + \dfrac{i_{\text{bias}}}{e_b}\right)}{\log \epsilon}$$

Let $\Delta t = RC$. Then

$$\log \epsilon = -\log \frac{R}{2}\left(\frac{1}{R_N} + \frac{i_{\text{bias}}}{e_b}\right)$$

or

$$\frac{1}{\epsilon} = \frac{R}{2}\left(\frac{1}{R_N} + \frac{i_{\text{bias}}}{e_b}\right)$$

or

$$i_{\text{bias}} = \left(\frac{2}{\epsilon R} - \frac{1}{R_N}\right) e_b$$

Let $R_N = 10R$. Then

$$i_{\text{bias}} = \left(\frac{2}{\epsilon} - \frac{1}{10}\right)\frac{e_b}{R} = 0.635 \, \frac{e_b}{R}$$

$$R_{\text{bias}} = \frac{15}{i_{\text{bias}}} = \frac{15R}{0.635 e_b}$$

Trigger equation:

$$\frac{E_T - 0.6}{R_S} \geqq i_{\text{bias}} - \frac{e_b}{R_N}$$

Then

$$R_S \leqq \frac{E_T - 0.6}{\dfrac{15}{R_{\text{bias}}} - \dfrac{e_b}{R_N}}$$

Example: Given $\Delta T = 1$ millisecond and $E_T = 1.6$ volt

Choose

$$C = 0.01 \text{ microfarad}$$

Then

$$R = \frac{\Delta t}{C} = \frac{10^{-3}}{10^{-8}} = 10^5 = 100K$$

Thus

$$R_N = 10R = 1 \, M$$

$$R_{\text{bias}} = \frac{15 \times 10^5}{0.635 \times 8} \cong 300K$$

$$R_S \leqq \frac{1.6 - 0.6}{\dfrac{15}{3 \times 10^5} - \dfrac{8}{10 \times 10^5}} = \frac{1}{5 - 0.8} \times 10^5 = 24K$$

Choose

$$R_S = 10K$$

$$R_T = R_S = 10K$$

$$C_T = 0.001 \text{ microfarad}$$

Thus

$$R_T C_T = \frac{RC}{100}$$

Figure 13.26. Design Procedure and Specimen Design of Figure 13.25.

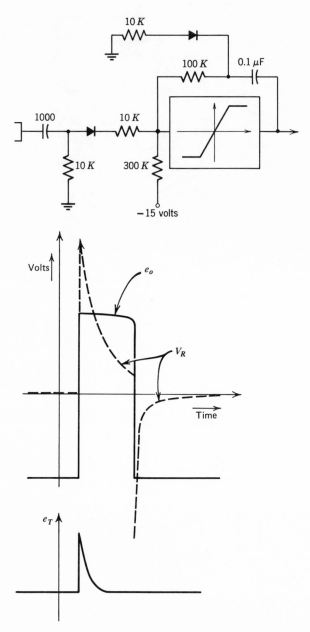

Figure 13.27. One-shot multivibrator modified for quick recovery.

If a dc feedback path is connected around a freerunning multivibrator, the circuit becomes bistable and will remain permanently in either of its two states. The resistor R_2 in Figure 13.28 is such a path. When the path is momentarily interrupted, the circuit reverts to its freerunning

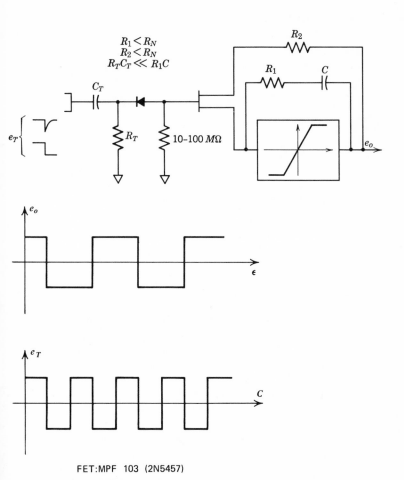

FET:MPF 103 (2N5457)

Figure 13.28. Bistable multivibrator (counting flip-flop).

mode and immediately makes a transition to the other state. If the interruption is over before the period of one half cycle the circuit remains in the other state. The F.E.T. in the figure serves as a momentary switch to open the resistive feedback on receipt of a negative pulse or negative-going transition. For each such input event the circuit changes its output state. This enormously useful behavior has several names. The circuit is called a binary counter or a counting flip-flop; it is also called a frequency divider because when driven by a square wave it produces a second square wave of exactly half the repetition frequency. The waveforms in the figure illustrate this property, which comes about because the circuit changes state in response to negative transitions only. Another way to think of this circuit is as a single-bit binary memory. This is modest storage indeed by digital standards, yet makes possible a surprising amount of automatic manipulation.

If the F.E.T. switch is controlled on a dc basis rather than a pulse basis there results a gated square-wave generator that is inherently synchronized with the gating signal. Such a circuit is ideally suited for use with the circuit of Figure 12.27 to make a staircase generator free of any timing problem. A driver circuit such as Figure 13.16 is all that is required to control the F.E.T.

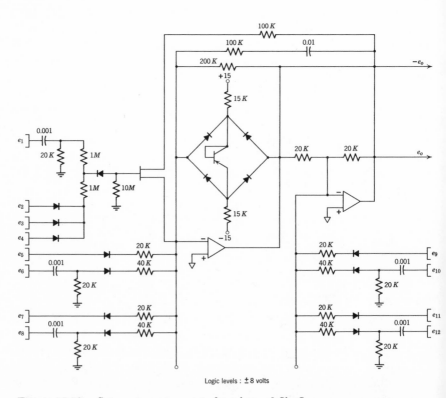

Logic levels : ± 8 volts

Figure 13.29.   Set-reset arrangements for triggered flip-flop.

The bistable triggerable multivibrator given here has very great generality as a logical element. By appropriate connections to its two operational summing points, great flexibility and complexity of logical function may be achieved; some of these possibilities are indicated in Figure 13.29. Logic levels of $+$ and $-$ 8 volts are assumed, which implies that 16-volt pulses result from differentiation of the transitions, a fact that must be kept in mind in designing circuits to operate logically with levels and pulses together. A negative event applied to input 1 will momentarily shut off the F.E.T. and cause triggering, except when a high level is present on any of the inputs 2, 3, or 4. Due to the 2:1 voltage divider formed by the 1-megohm resistors, the pulse is unable to shut the F.E.T. off when the positive level signal is present. Any of the inputs 2–4 may be thought of as inhibiting the trigger when they are high. A high level at input 5 will force the output e_o to be high, so long as the input is present. Input 5 might be called a direct set input. Conversely, a high level at input 9 forces the output to be low, which entitles it to be called a direct reset input. In the same scheme of terminology input 6 is an ac set input and 10 is an ac reset input for positive events. The remaining inputs serve analogously for low levels and negative events. Clearly not all of the inputs shown would be needed in any given case, but the figure illustrates that set-reset capability exists for all situations.

It should be understood that incomparably superior hardware abounds in the digital arsenal; these circuits are offered here principally because that arsenal is so vast and formidable. It is hoped that the relative simplicity and predictability of these switching circuits will encourage the assembly of automated instruments and systems of small scale, for it is here that the considerable promise of cybernetics has not been realized.

Chapter XIV

Operational Systems

An operational system is an aggregation of operational circuits that performs a special function, usually as part of a larger engineering system. It handles operational variables primarily, but contains control logic internal to itself, and may include provision for interfacing with digital or other external equipment.

This chapter is the culmination of all the techniques that have gone before, which though valuable in themselves will be seen to acquire new utility as parts of these autonomous systems. Due to the relative complexity and the self-excited nature of these systems, it is recommended that they initially be connected exactly as in the schematic diagram and set to work. This provides a reference configuration to which the desired modifications can be made systematically; numerical values are provided in the schematics for this purpose.

The first system is a precise repetitive ramp or sawtooth generator, voltage controlled in that an external reference voltage can set the slope of the ramp function and hence the number of ramps per unit time, since the reset time is a small fraction of the cycle time at all but the highest operating rates. See Figures 14.1 and 14.2. The idea of generating precise ramps by integrating a constant reference voltage is now familiar; the heart of this system is the hysteresis circuit that governs the resetting of the integrator. It is salutary to first consider a simpler system, so simple that it does not work, to elicit the reason for its failure. The defective system obtains when the hysteresis circuit is replaced by a biased voltage crossing detector. See Figure 14.3. When

208

the system is first energized the output of the integrator ramps positively until it crosses the bias voltage of the crossing detector, which switches and causes the logic driver to close the reset switch; so far all is well. The integrator starts to reset to zero, but as soon as its output crosses the bias level the crossing detector switches back, starting the integration once again. The result is that the circuit multivibrates at small amplitude around the bias level, as shown in the time history. A first thought as to what is needed is a delay in the opening of the reset switch after it has once been closed, the delay giving the integrator time enough to reset to zero. Indeed, sawtooth generators are built in this way; it works well for a fixed repetition rate or for a small range of repetition rates.

The sawtooth generator of Figures 14.1 and 14.2 operates over a range of more than 1000 in repetition rate. It is enabled to do so by the hysteresis circuit, which keeps the reset switch closed until the output has completely reset and then opens it immediately to start a new ramp. For convenience it will be assumed that the bounded amplifier in the hysteresis circuit is bounded at ± 7.5 volts or half of the 15-volt supply voltage. In Figure 14.1 is a plot of the output of the hysteresis circuit as a function of the system output or sawtooth voltage; it illustrates what may be called the switching trajectories of the system. The plot is derived from the hysteresis loop plot of Figure 13.12 by taking into account the currents in R_1, R_2, and R_3. Resistor R_1 provides a bias that shifts the loop to the right of the origin. The action may be taken to start at point 1 with the beginning of the integration of the ramp. The output moves positive steadily at a rate proportional to the reference voltage until it crosses 10 volts at point 2. At this output voltage the current through R_3 overbalances the currents through R_1 and R_2 and regenerative switching occurs, taking the operating point promptly to point 3. The logic driver circuit causes the F.E.T. switch to conduct, and as current through the F.E.T. discharges the integrating capacitor the output drops toward point 4 on the trajectory. At the end of the reset action the capacitor is discharged and the current to the summing point through the 100K resistor is simply shorted to the output by the F.E.T. However, at point 4, which is a few millivolts above ground potential, the hysteresis circuit switches regeneratively back to point 1, opening the reset switch and releasing the integrator to repeat the cycle. There is thus a causal sequence that depends only on *what* has happened and is independent of how fast it happens.

Point 4 must be slightly positive to insure switching because the integrator resets only to zero. The 10K resistor shown in series with R_2 serves to make sure that the system will run when first connected. It

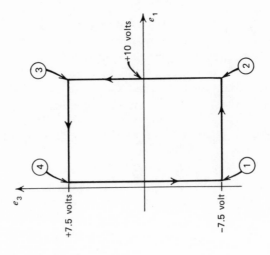

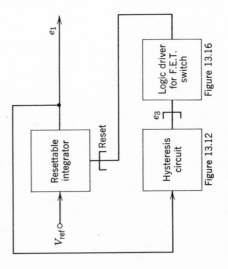

Figure 14.1. Sawtooth generator.

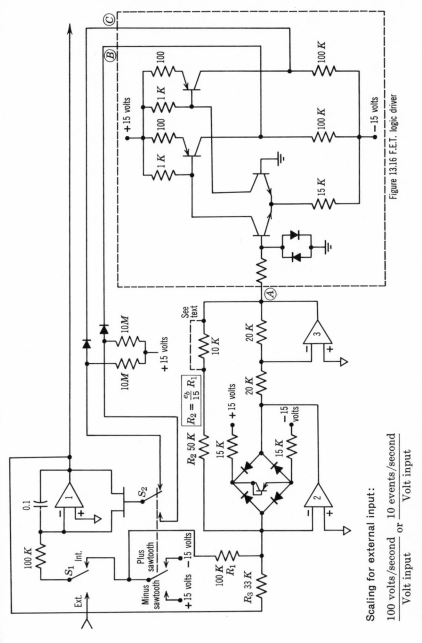

Figure 13.16 F.E.T. logic driver

Scaling for external input:

$$\frac{100 \text{ volts/second}}{\text{Volt input}} \quad \text{or} \quad \frac{10 \text{ events/second}}{\text{Volt input}}$$

Figure 14.2. Sawtooth-generator schematic.

$$R_2 = \frac{e_b}{15} R_1$$

211

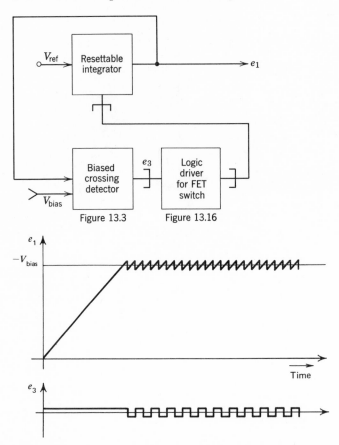

Figure 14.3.   An unsuccessful sawtooth generator.

should be trimmed down to a low value, thus moving point 4 close to zero from above, and giving a 10-volt sawtooth wave.

The schematic provides for switch selectable negative or positive sawtooth waves, and for internal or external reference voltage.

It is fair to conclude that systems employing the hysteresis circuit are somewhat demanding conceptually, although they can be shown to be economical of hardware. A large part of the difficulty arises from the cyclic nature of such systems; those which depend on an external event to make them go are inherently much easier to understand.

The next assemblage is almost too simple in concept to be called a system, yet it meets the definition and performs a function not easily duplicated. See Figures 14.4 and 14.5. It produces bursts of precise sine

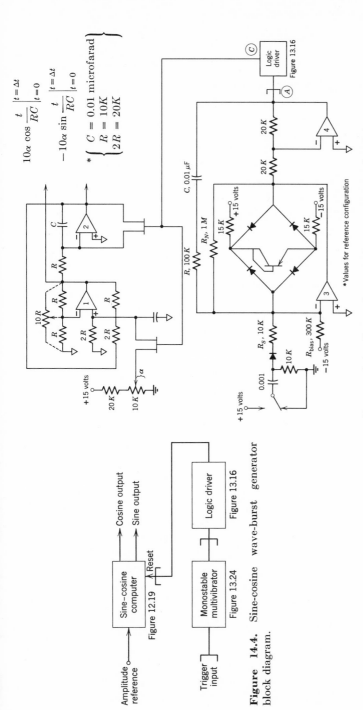

$$10\alpha \cos \frac{t}{RC}\bigg|_{t=0}^{t=\Delta t}$$

$$-10\alpha \sin \frac{t}{RC}\bigg|_{t=0}^{t=\Delta t}$$

$$*\begin{cases} C = 0.01 \text{ microfarad} \\ R = 10K \\ 2R = 20K \end{cases}$$

*Values for reference configuration

Figure 14.5. Sine-cosine wave-burst generator schematic.

Figure 14.4. Sine-cosine wave-burst generator block diagram.

213

and cosine waves, the time duration of the burst being set by a one-shot multivibrator, which resets the integrators to terminate the event. The potentiometer shown by dashed lines enables the wave train to be adjusted for exponential growth or decay from the amplitude set by the initial condition voltage on the first integrator.

The next system had its origin in the need for an easily made adjustment of the period of a one-shot multivibrator—working even briefly with the system above will demonstrate this need. As in other cases ease of adjustment and voltage control are nearly synonymous in the outcome. The final system has another property that was not anticipated during its design evolution; its active period is directly proportional to a reference voltage and inversely proportional to a second reference voltage; it is in fact proportional to the *quotient* of the references and very precisely so. When this property can be exploited, which obviously is not often, it may obviate an electronic divider. The corollary properties of either direct or inverse response to an external voltage should find more frequent application.

Another design objective was the generation of precise timing intervals in excess of 100 seconds. It is appreciated that epoch demarcation on this scale under precise voltage control may not be a universal need.

The block diagram of Figure 14.6 shows the system to be an operational integrator under the reset control of a set-reset bistable multivibrator. The action is started by applying a trigger event to the flip-flop, which changes state and releases the integrator to generate a precise ramp by integrating $e_{ref\ 2}$. When the ramp voltage crosses $e_{ref\ 1}$ the crossing detector switches state and this transition resets the flip-flop, which in turn resets the integrator to zero, restoring the initial state. In addition to the switching variable output conventional to a multivibrator, this system also provides a precise ramp the slope of which is proportional to $e_{ref\ 2}$, and the active period of which is proportional to the quotient of the reference voltages as noted above. In defiance of a long and obtuse tradition this system is named a *monovibrator*.

The schematic of Figure 14.7 is a straightforward implementation of the block diagram, with the exception of the crossing detector (amplifier 2), which has been modified to switch sharply even for the very slow input changes that obtain when the system is applied as a long-epoch demarcator. It is conventional to add "snap action" to a crossing detector by feeding a fraction of the output back to the direct input, but this scheme has the disadvantage of an imprecise hysteresis loop surrounding the nominal switching point. This difficulty is avoided here by disconnecting the positive feedback by means of a diode for inputs approaching the switching point from below. The hysteresis loop is thus shifted to the reset portion of the cycle where it does not affect the accuracy. (It does place a lower limit on the magnitude of reference voltage $e_{ref\ 1}$, below which the crossing detector will not switch back because of the hysteresis. If this is intolerable the positive feedback should be disconnected since it is needed only for long timing period service.) The system may be changed to produce negative ramps by inverting the diodes, the zener substitute, the reference voltages, and the logic driver in rather self-evident—but not trivial—ways; the logic of operational systems is every bit as inexorable as that familiar to the user of digital machines.

Figure 14.8 is the configuration of a triangular wave generator upon which the next six systems are based. It appears on page 71 of the Philbrick/Nexus *Applications Manual for Operational Amplifiers*, and is the handiwork of Robert A. Pease. The heart of the system is the diode switch that allows currents of selected polarity to flow. The magnitude of these currents is determined by the reference voltages and by the resistors (if the forward drop of the conducting diode is ignored, which drop will be compensated in the refined versions to follow). The current paths illustrating how the switch is toggled by the driving amplifier are detailed in the figure, giving a picture of the action that is sufficient to understand it. Note how the blocking diodes in each case are forcefully back-biased.

To explain self-excited systems of this sort it is conventional to pick a point in the endlessly repeating cycle and explain one's way around it until the starting point is reached again. Although the cycle does not have a defined end, the system behavior must have a beginning, following on its being energized, and an explication from the start-up point will be given here in the hope of preventing the intellectual queasy feeling that so often accompanies indulgence in the conventional rationale: when power is applied to the system of Figure 14.8, it is conceivable that current divides equally in the diode bridges and that an equilibrium comes about in which amplifier input and output voltages are zero and have zero rate of change. Such an equilibrium is a fragile affair, however. Suppose that one of the diodes of the bridge on the left, for example, D_6, becomes momentarily and infinitesimally more conductive than the others, perhaps as the result of a hit from a fragment of a cosmic ray shower. The result is that net current is delivered to the direct input of amplifier 1, raising its voltage, and hence that of the output. It should now become clear that the diode bridge will become progressively and regeneratively unbalanced because in effect a positive feedback loop has been connected which promptly drives amplifier 1 to its positive bound, and which sets amplifier 2 integrating in the nega-

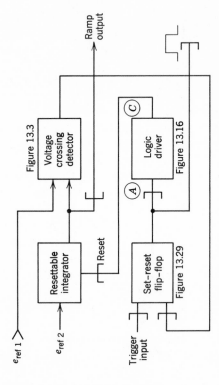

Figure 14.6. Voltage-ratio-controlled monovibrator block diagram.

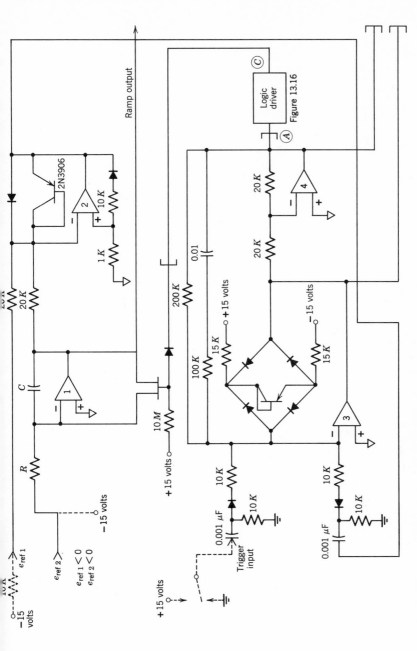

Figure 14.7. Voltage-ratio-controlled monovibrator.

217

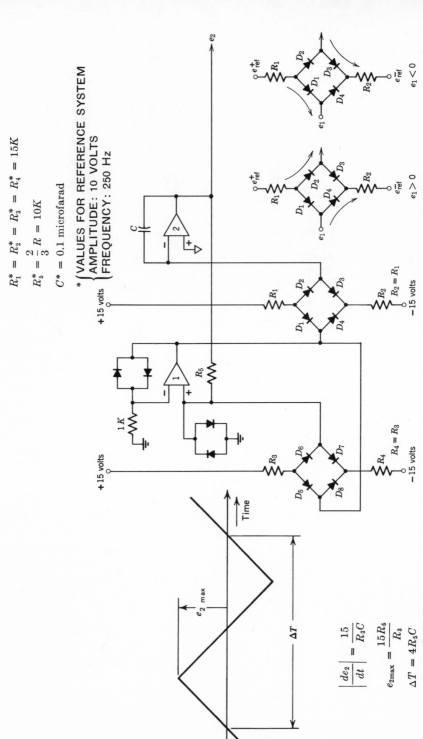

$R_1^* = R_2^* = R_3^* = R_4^* = 15K$

$R_5^* = \frac{2}{3} R = 10K$

$C^* = 0.1$ microfarad

$* \begin{cases} \text{VALUES FOR REFERENCE SYSTEM} \\ \text{AMPLITUDE: 10 VOLTS} \\ \text{FREQUENCY: 250 Hz} \end{cases}$

$e_1 < 0$

$e_1 > 0$

$\left| \dfrac{de_2}{dt} \right| = \dfrac{15}{R_3 C}$

$e_{2max} = \dfrac{15 R_5}{R_3}$

$\Delta T = 4 R_5 C$

Figure 14.8. Basic triangular-wave generator. Values for reference system: amplitude, 10 volts; frequency, 250 hertz.

218

tive direction in response to current through R_1 and D_2. This state of affairs continues until the output of 2 reaches approximately -10 volts. The current through R_5 then is equal and opposite to the current through R_3, and the direct input of 1 relaxes to zero volts and beyond. Once the direct input of 1 crosses zero volts and goes negative, regenerative switching occurs and everything reverses, with the integrator output heading toward a similar appointment at the $+10$-volt level.

Amplifier 1 is a crossing detector which switches its own reference polarity as well as that of the integrator input current. The slope of the triangular wave and hence its period are easily deduced from the component values, and are given by the formulae in the figure. Switching the integrating capacitor is a convenient way of making gross changes in the operating speed, decade changes being typical.

Having achieved a system that runs literally like clockwork—its principle is used in cardiac pacemakers—the next step is to modify it so that, most unlike a clock, it responds to external stimuli. The next system allows convenient adjustment of the triangular wave frequency by means of a linear potentiometer. More significantly it provides *frequency modulation* of the triangular wave by an external voltage. The frequency modulation involved here is of a very pure sort; the frequency is directly proportional to the command voltage over a range exceeding 1000:1. See Figure 14.9. The voltage references for the integrator are supplied by amplifiers 3 and 4 in response either to the setting of a calibrated dial or to an external programming voltage. Amplifier 3 compensates for the forward voltage drop of diodes D_2 and D_3 by augmenting its output voltage by the drop of D_{23}, a matched diode. Diode D_{23} is operated at a matching current because the resistor in series with it is equal to those in series with the bridge diodes. This artifice is used throughout the systems that follow, and is responsible for their dynamic range and temperature stability. Since it is practical to match diodes within 10 millivolts and to mount them in thermal propinquity, dynamic ranges of controllability exceeding 1000:1 can be achieved, given careful attention to other error sources. For extreme dynamic range, diode-connected silicon transistors should be substituted for the diodes, as indicated in the figure. Amplifier 4 simply inverts the output of 3, including the diode offset correction. The effect of modulating the integrator input currents in this way is to modulate the slopes of the triangular wave. This is tantamount to frequency modulation because the amplitude of the wave is fixed by the crossing detector.

Applying the same tactic to the crossing-detector reference current produces a triangular wave modulable as to its amplitude and, more importantly, as to its period. See Figure 14.10. If the output of amplifier

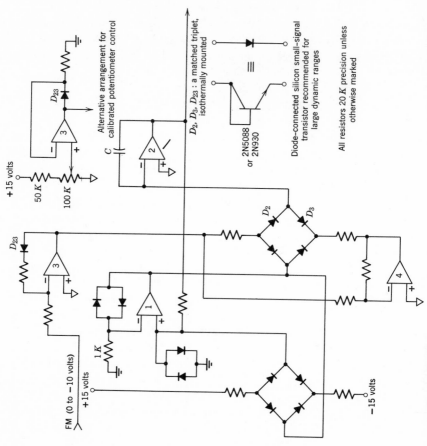

Alternative arrangement for calibrated potentiometer control

D_{23}

+15 volts

50 K

100 K

C

2

D_2, D_3, D_{23} : a matched triplet, isothermally mounted

2N5088 or 2N930

Diode-connected silicon small-signal transistor recommended for large dynamic ranges

All resistors 20 K precision unless otherwise marked

D_{23}

3

D_2

D_3

1

4

FM (0 to −10 volts)

+15 volts

1 K

−15 volts

220

Figure 14.9   Frequency modulation [LLLA, 1]

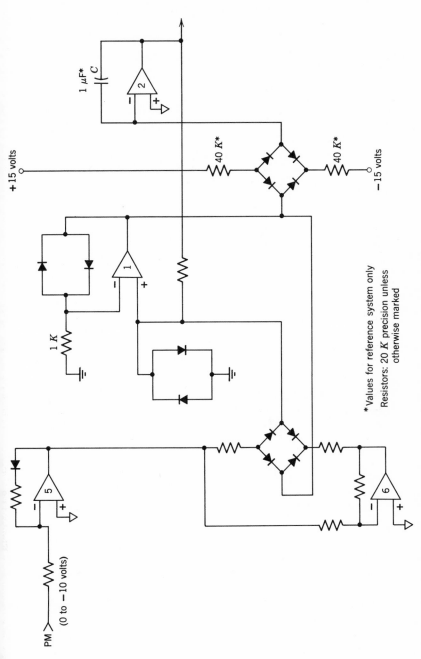

Figure 14.10. Period-modulated triangular-wave generator (voltage-controlled).

*Values for reference system only
Resistors: 20 K precision unless otherwise marked

221

1 or 2 is fed into an unbiased bounded amplifier there results a square wave the period or cycle time of which is directly proportional to the programming voltage. This system may serve as the transmitting encoder of a very low frequency data-transmission link, described in more detail below in connection with the receiver or decoder system (Figures 14.21–14.23).

It was remarked that amplitude modulation was a byproduct of the period modulation that was sought. A more desirable form of amplitude modulation that does not affect the nominal frequency can be arranged by combining the two previous systems. See Figure 14.11. Reference voltages of perhaps −5 volts each are connected to the FM and PM inputs, establishing a nominal triangular wave of 5-volt amplitude. By operational addition the AM input signal alters the reference level of the crossing detector and in compensatory fashion alters the slope of the triangular wave, thus keeping the frequency approximately constant. Unfortunately the AM output is not suited for shaping into a sine wave, which restricts its utility in comparison with the FM version and the two-phase and phase-modulated versions below. On the other hand, the amplitude modulation does not interact or conflict with the various other forms (except period modulation) and thus may well be included in systems in which a triangular wave carrier is acceptable or desirable, as it is in many automatic test or check-out systems.

The next system gives two triangular waves 90° apart in phase. When shaped into sinusoids by circuits similar to Figure 12.25, these waves may be operated on by the phase-variation circuit of Figure 12.22 to give sources of sine waves easily variable as to frequency and phase (but not voltage-controlled in phase). A sounder approach to the generation of variable-phase sinusoids is the variable-phase triangular-wave generator (voltage-controlled), to which this two-phase system is a necessary introduction. The point of departure for the evolution of the biphase system was the observation that the triangular wave was shifted precisely one-quarter of a cycle from the rough square wave that is the output of the crossing detector (amplifier 1). This of course follows from the manner of operation of the basic system in which switching of the detector causes reversal of the integrator and thus is synchronous with the peaks of the triangular wave. Put another way, if the triangular wave output is fed into a bounded amplifier the resulting square wave is shifted 90° from the crossing-detector square wave. In Figure 14.12 where this is done, the output of 7 is 90° behind the output of 1. The idea was to run a second switched integrator off the output of 7, to give a second triangular wave 90° behind the first—if some means could be found to stabilize the average dc level of this otherwise freerunning

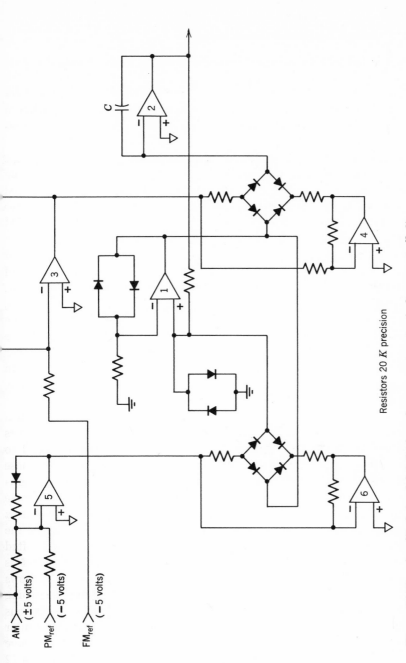

Figure 14.11. Amplitude-modulated triangular-wave generator (voltage-controlled).

Resistors 20 K precision

AM (±5 volts)

PM_ref (−5 volts)

FM_ref (−5 volts)

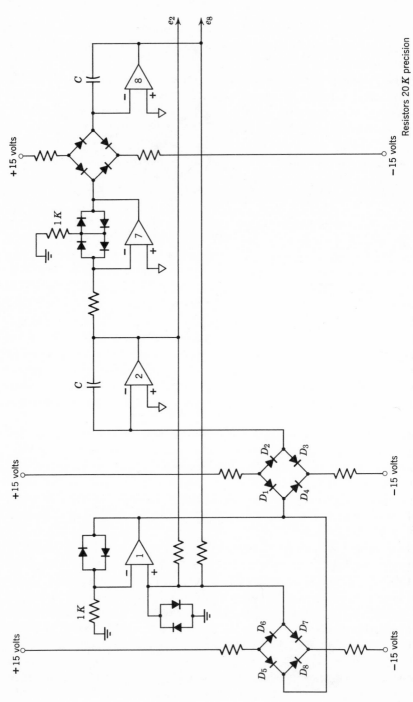

Figure 14.12. Basic two-phase triangular-wave generator.

integrator. That is, there were questions as to how such a system would start up and as to what would result from the inevitable slight differences in integration rate up versus down of the second integrator. Various schemes occurred for extracting the average dc level of the second triangle so that it might be correctively fed back. There are two objections to them all: (1) filtering and feedback are uneasy companions because of the phase shift associated with the filtering, and (2) it was desired that the scheme work for even the lowest frequencies, and that there be no long period of stabilization after a change in the input.

A solution was found with remarkable ease based on the idea that, because of the desired 90° phase relation, zero-crossings of the second wave should be synchronous with the peaks of the first, which are the critical points that determine when the crossing detector switches. Thus if the second triangular wave is correctly zero at the critical instant during which the switching decision is made, as it were, by the crossing detector, then feeding the second wave back directly should not influence the decision. It remained to be ascertained that a nonzero value of the second wave would influence the decision correctively, as in fact it does when fed back in the manner of Figure 14.12; an invertor would otherwise have been employed. The resulting system makes its decision about when to switch depend on the instantaneous sum of the two triangular waves; it splits the difference between the two outputs. Here is an example of a lucky success, a partially formed idea that was tried and that worked. A more circumspect analysis, derived in the aftermath, is given below. For all of the luck involved, and without in any way condoning blind experimentation, it should be remarked that it was the flexibility of the electronic medium that made this experiment feasible. Had the medium been mechanical or hydraulic no such casual experiment could have been attempted, and not only would the route to the result have been much longer, there is a strong presumption that it would not have been taken at all. More will be said about prudent experimentation in the final chapter.

It is useful to narrate the behavior of the biphase system beginning from the moment it is energized, although the largely hypothetical unstable equilibrium will be passed over and amplifier 1 taken to go immediately to its positive bound. See Figure 14.13. Because the output of amplifier 1 is positive, diode D_2 conducts and amplifier 2 ramps in the negative direction, causing the output of 7 to be positive, and thus causing 8 to also ramp in the negative direction. The two outputs are initially superposed until their sum, the dashed line in the figure, touches the crossing-detector threshold level, at which point amplifier 1 switches, reversing amplifier 2. Amplifier 8 continues to ramp downward until

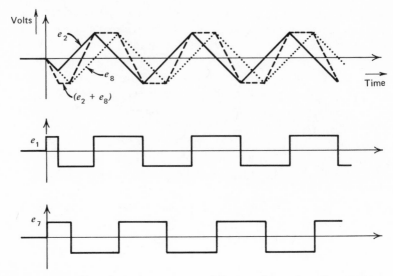

Figure 14.13.   Wave forms from start-up of the two-phase triangular-wave generator (see Figure 14.12).

2 crosses zero, causing 7 to switch and 8 to reverse. Once this last event has occurred the desired 90° phase relation is established and is thereafter maintained. There is thus a tidy determinism about the action; if amplifier 1 happens to go initially to its negative bound the entire process takes place in mirror image with the same result, amplifier 8 lagging 90° behind 2. The writer takes such delight in this process that he is not tempted to imply that he planned it that way.

The peak points of amplifier 8 are set by the zero crossings of 2—this at least was planned—and the peak points of 2 are set by the crossing-detector threshold and by the sum of the outputs of 2 and 8. To illustrate the self-regulating property of these machinations, Figure 14.14 traces out how the system recovers from a step error in the output of 8.

The scheme for varying the phase of the second triangular wave begins with the notion of applying a bias to amplifier 7 so that it switches not on the zero crossings of the first wave but at other points in the cycle. The first complication arises because it is not sufficient to apply bias of the same polarity during both halves of the cycle. The bias, like other quantities in this system, must be switched in synchronism with the output of amplifier 1; thus a third diode switch driven by 1, along with two amplifiers to set the bias voltage and its negative, are required. These amplifiers are designated 9 and 10 in Figure 14.15.

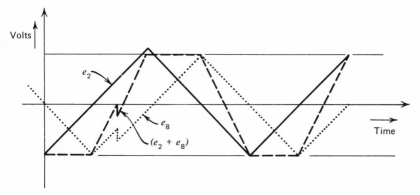

Figure 14.14.   Response of system to a step error.

A second complication arises because bias of both polarities is required in order to permit the command of a phase lead as well a phase lag in the second triangular wave. Thus the diode switch must be capable of handling currents of either polarity during both parts of its cycle, which the four diode switch simply cannot do. For this reason an eight-diode switch is required along with a transistor logic inverter to drive the outer ring of diodes. These complications are no more than that and are handled adequately by the circuitry given in Figure 14.15. An operational invertor can replace the little transistor circuit if this is expedient, although the $1K$ resistors should be inserted between the bridges and the driving amplifier outputs to avoid a short circuit condition.

A final consideration is fundamental: if the second triangular wave is to have a phase other than $90°$ behind the first, then its instantaneous value will no longer be zero when the switching decision for reversing the first wave is being made. This simply means that the threshold for the crossing detector, amplifier 1, must be adjusted accordingly. Because the waves are triangular all of the relationships are linear and in practice all that is required is accomplished by the resistor connected from the phase-modulation input terminal to the summing point of amplifier 5. If the reader finds all this less than blindingly clear, he is assured that the fault is not his and that here is no great matter; those who need phase modulation will readily enough puzzle out how this circuit makes it possible. Plus and minus $90°$ of relative shift are available in response to voltages applied to the phase-modulation input, allowing the second wave to range from being in phase to being $180°$ behind the first. Note that amplifier 9 is equipped with compensating diodes

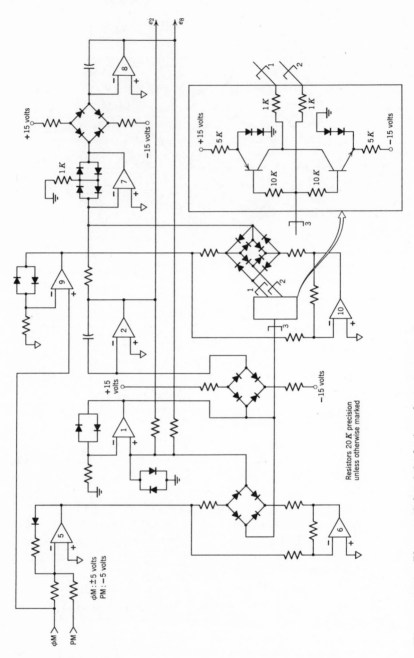

Figure 14.15. Phase-modulated dual triangular-wave generator.

facing in both directions because it must handle bipolar signals. The amplifier output jumps as it goes through zero, but the diode compensation philosophy holds even through the zero crossing and there is no corresponding jump in the phase of the output.

The final fully modulable system appears in Figure 14.16. If a constant —5-volt reference is applied to the PM input, the others, which do not interact, may be modulated at will. An oscilloscope cross plot of the two outputs is of interest although it does not reveal the frequency modulation except at the very low rates where the phosphor persistence does not obscure it. Multibeam or multitrace scopes are also pertinent to displaying this system in action, although care should not be lacking to keep separate the science from the fiction.

The foregoing system entails no more than about $20 in microcircuit amplifiers and perhaps slightly more in precision resistors, depending on the tolerance. It is entirely reasonable to consider it as a general laboratory instrument of wide utility, small size and cost, and high reliability.

When the amplitude is set to an accurate 10 volts, the outputs of the FM phase-modulated version may be fed to commercially available devices specially designed for shaping triangular waves into sine waves and costing under $100 apiece. The prices are as of January 1971. If amplitude modulation of the resulting frequency-modulated, phase-modulated sinusoids is demanded, then a pair of analog multipliers is indicated, as is perhaps a vacation for the system planner.

Somewhat in the spirit of comic relief after this concatenation of heavy machinery, the next item isn't a system at all, but rather an amusing gadget for converting all these triangles into passable pseudosinusoids, sine waves pure enough at least that most people cannot *hear* the difference. It has the serious purpose as well of enabling a preliminary test of these various generators in terms of ultimate sine-wave outputs, without requiring the shaping circuits mentioned above. The waveform is in fact good enough for a great many purposes, being comparable to that of a garden-variety oscillator that has not been serviced recently, and the amplitude and frequency stability are substantially better when used on the output of any of these generators. The gadget, which appears in Figure 14.17, has the additional virtue of serving as an adjustable gain-output amplifier since the nonlinear goodies are confined to the forward path. Its operation will not be explained because it is comically obvious to the electronicist and of no interest to anyone else.

An adjustment circuit is given in Figure 14.18 for setting up these shaping circuits to emulate a proper sine wave. The amplitude of the triangular wave is fixed at something in the range of 1 to 3 volts. Then

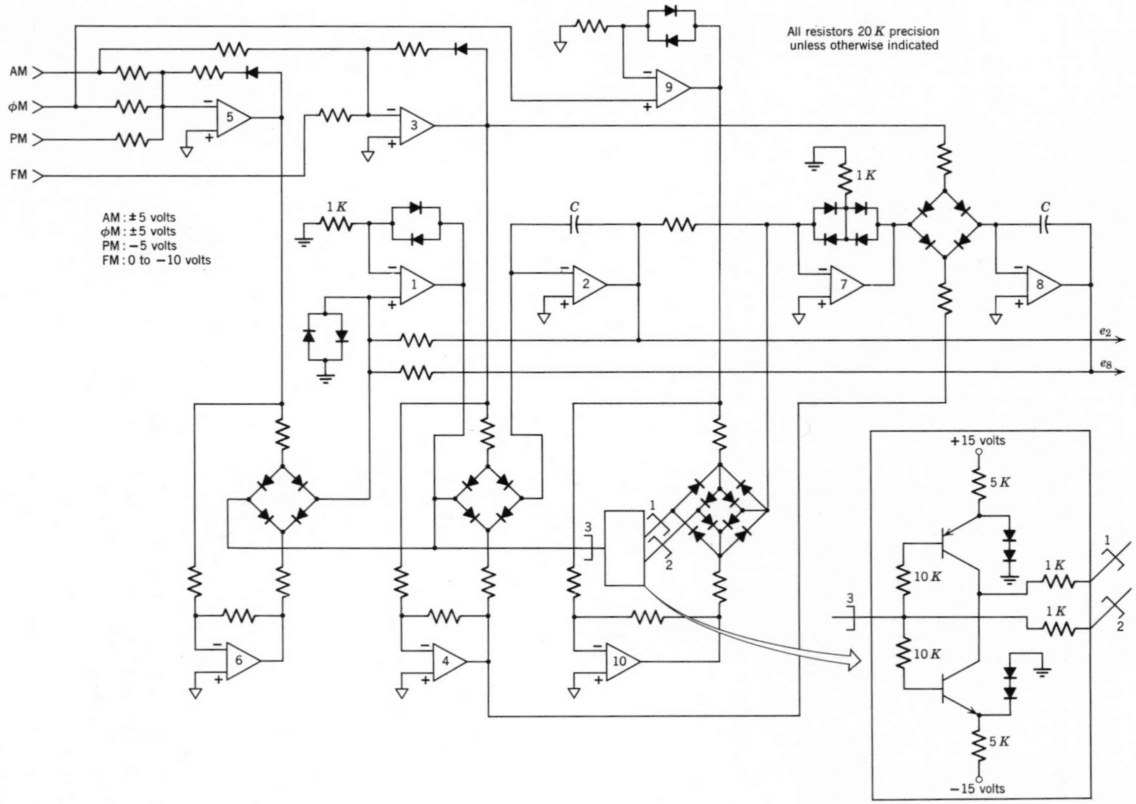
All resistors 20 K precision
unless otherwise indicated
AM
φM
PM
FM
AM : ±5 volts
φM : ±5 volts
PM : −5 volts
FM : 0 to −10 volts
1 K
C
e2
e8
+15 volts
5 K
10 K
1 K
−15 volts
1
2
3
4
5
6
7
8
9
10

Figure 14.16. Universal voltage-controlled triangular-wave generator.

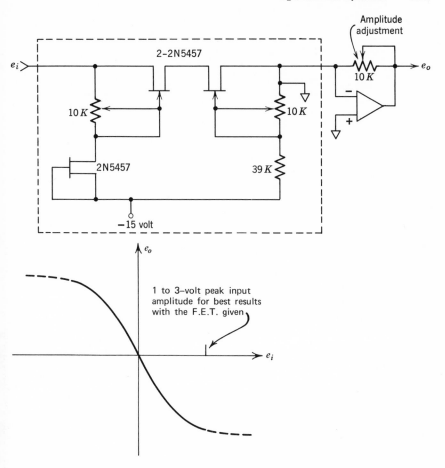

Figure 14.17. Approximate triangular-to-sine shaping circuit and output amplifier.

the frequency of the triangular wave is adjusted to be nearly equal to that of the sine-cosine generator, thus producing a nearly stationary Lissajous figure on the oscilloscope. The $100K$ rheostat is then connected as indicated and adjusted to just cause synchronization of the triangular wave with the sine wave. Then the frequency control of the triangular wave generator is touched up to adjust the relative phase to zero or $90°$ as desired. The various patterns in the chart will be visible as the various combinations of signals are displayed. The linear display is best for critical adjustment of the shaping circuit, with the circular pattern as a check, giving reassurance that this contrivance actually works.

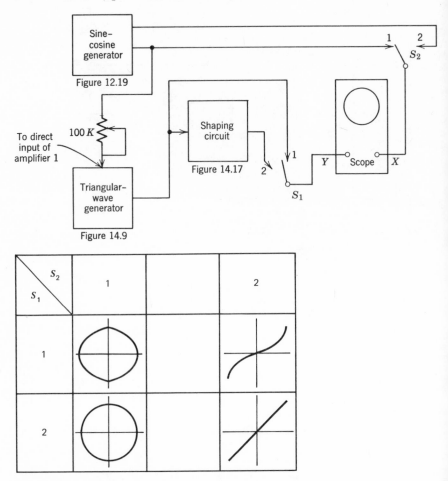

Figure 14.18. Adjustment technique for shaping circuit.

The compensated diode switch used in the triangular-wave systems can be applied elsewhere; its speed in particular commends it. It can be used to transform the output of an accurate and therefore expensive function generator from one-quadrant into two-quadrant service. The trigonometric functions provide examples of a large class of functions that exist symmetrically about the origin in the first and third quadrants. Figures 14.19 and 14.20 show how such a function is synthesized from its embodiment in a one-quadrant generator. The simple absolute value circuit shown is best adapted to functions like power laws that have

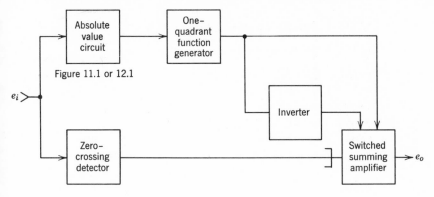

Figure 14.19. The inverse absolute value problem.

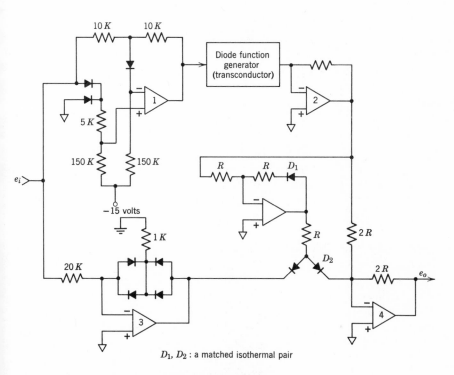

D_1, D_2 : a matched isothermal pair

Figure 14.20. The inverse absolute value problem.

233

zero slope at the origin, because the rounding error is thus of no concern. Functions like the sine or tangent are better served by the precision absolute value circuit of Figure 11.1 or a circuit based on the first half of Figure 13.5; the latter option is particularly attractive when the function is generated by a diode function transconductor to be located in a feedback path.

It was remarked in connection with the period or cycle-time modulated generator of Figure 14.10 that it could be used as the transmitting encoder of a very low frequency data-transmission link. The idea is to put variable period square waves of current into a rather low-quality land line of the type used for teletype signals. The period of signals ranging in frequency from 200 hertz to perhaps 10 hertz signifies the magnitude of the data quantity. A decoder is required having as a salient feature that its instantaneous output voltage shall be proportional to the duration of the last completed half cycle of the received signal. It can be shown that such a period detector has significant advantages over frequency counting schemes. The system to be described next also applies directly to measuring the period of very low frequency sources in minimum elapsed time. Figures 14.21 and 14.22 give the block diagram and waveforms of the system. The basic idea is to start an integrator running each time the input signal crosses zero and to put it into hold upon the occurrence of the next alternation. The value held by the integrator is then a measure of the semiperiod just completed, because the integrator input is an accurately known reference voltage. Since the frequencies are low it can be assumed that the integrator can be reset in zero time. Thus two integrators are required, one holding and the other integrating up from zero after having been reset by a very short pulse; see the lower-most waveform. It may then be seen that the only further required step is to take the upper envelope of the outputs of the integrators, which is done by the upper selector circuit. Thus not only is the output proportional to the elapsed time of the most recently completed half cycle, but it is proportional to the elapsed time of the semiperiod in progress when the data signal is growing. When the data signal is decreasing the automatic reset of the integrator reveals the lower value computed most recently by the other integrator. Thus the output may be said to reflect the period most recently completed, or the elapsed time of the period in progress if that is greater. It should be understood that the system is not intended to handle data with anything like the high-frequency content shown in the illustration.

The reference system schematized in Figure 14.23 will operate with the reference system of Figure 14.10 as a dc-to-dc data transmission system operating roughly between 10 and 200 hertz; negative dc signals applied to the PM input of the one will appear as positive signals of approximately the same magnitude at the output of the other. Rather than tightly specifying all the components it is easier to calibrate the system from end to end before deployment. Note that the system error may be easily measured as the voltage at the midpoint of a resistive divider between input and output.

The next system, a peak-sensitive amplitude demodulator, is roughly similar in configuration and in the hardware employed. Peak-reading detectors are attractive for several reasons, but have the disadvantage that they cannot read a series of peaks of *decreasing* amplitude. This system is able to do so and gives a full-wave peak-detected output because it comprises two peak followers linked by the logic system in such a way that they are reset to zero on alternate half cycles of the input signal. See Figures 14.24 and 14.25. The input signal is inverted before being fed to the lower peak follower, so that in effect it is a valley follower with respect to the input signal. Since a full-wave rectified output is sought it all comes out right in the end. The rate-crossing detector circuit is used here as a peak-event detector; transitions in its output occur as a result of peaks or valleys of the input signal and are used to command pulse reset of the appropriate peak follower. The output consists of the upper envelope of the outputs of the peak followers, obtained as before by submitting them to an upper selector circuit. It can be seen in the waveform chart in Figure 14.25 that each new peak is held by its own peak follower and causes reset of the other peak follower, which perforce had been holding the previous peak. Thus the system peak follows the input signal down as well as up. It should be intuitively clear that a minimum of filtering is required to "fill in the chinks" to restore the original form of the modulating signal. The schematic in Figure 14.26 requires no special comment; the system can be tried out in conjunction with the precise modulator of Figure 14.11.

An FM detection system is not given here because such frequency-to-voltage converters are widely published elsewhere.

The next system will be of practical interest to those who have an oscilloscope without dual-trace capability. See Figures 14.27 and 14.28. An operational switch selects between two inputs on alternate sweeps of the scope. A triggered flip-flop performs the mundane but vital task of alternating the states of the switch. It is triggered by a crossing detector of the noninverting variety used in the triangular-wave generators; the crossing detector operates on the sawtooth horizontal-deflection waveform available on the front panel of many oscilloscopes, especially

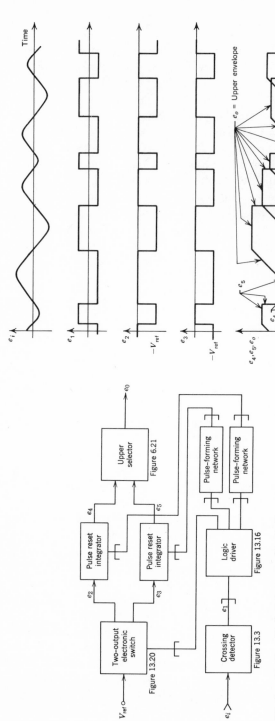

Figure 14.22. Period-detector waveforms.

Figure 14.21. Period-detector block diagram.

236

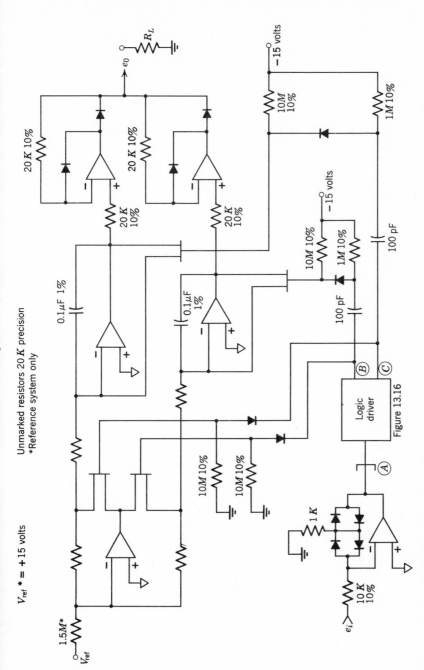

Figure 14.23. Period-detector schematic.

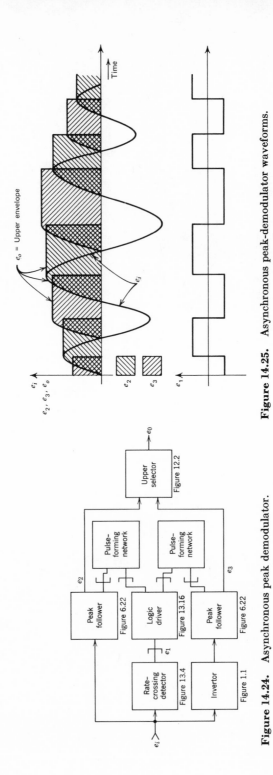

Figure 14.25. Asynchronous peak-demodulator waveforms.

Figure 14.24. Asynchronous peak demodulator.

238

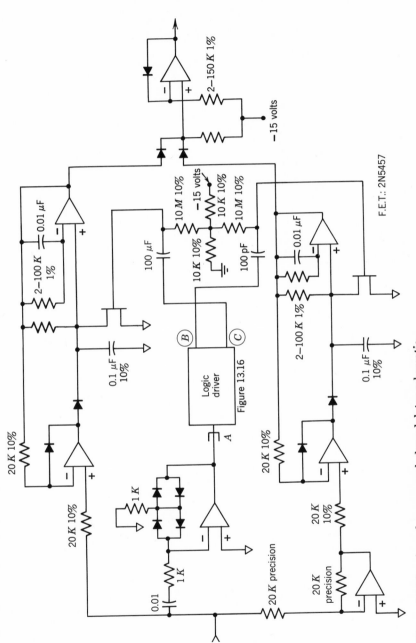

Figure 14.26. Asynchronous peak-demodulator schematic.

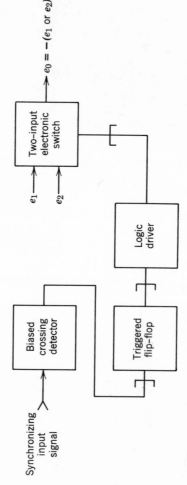

Figure 14.27.

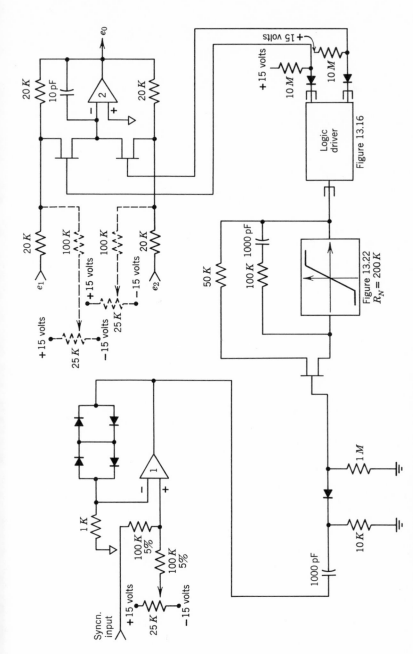

Figure 14.28. Two-position electronic scanning switch.

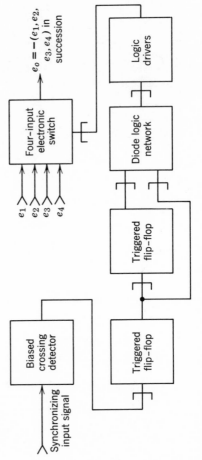

Figure 14.29. Four-position electronic scanning switch.

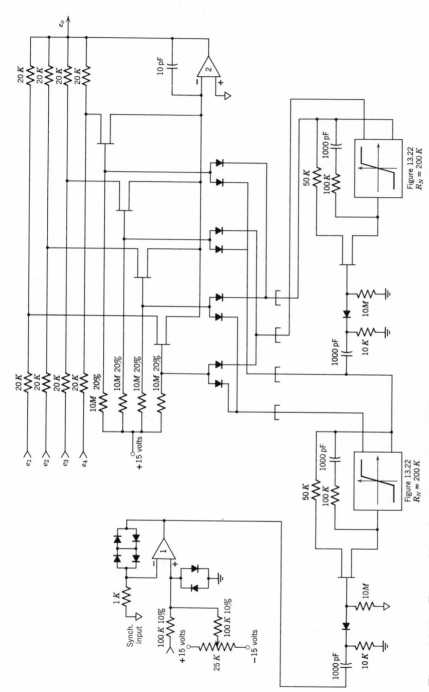

Figure 14.30. Four-position electronic scanning switch schematic.

the older types. The flip-flop is triggered by the return of the traditionally positive sawtooth at the end of the sweep. The bias potentiometer shown may not be necessary.

Because the oscilloscope controls the switch, rather than vice versa as in some commercial units, great convenience results for the user, with the oscilloscope behaving like a dual-beam machine except at the low sweep rates where the phosphor persistence will not support the illusion. The potentiometers shown in dashed lines are a convenient way of vertically displacing the traces from each other. Otherwise, if the two inputs are connected to the same signal, it will be seen that the switch is gratifyingly free of offset.

It was remarked in Chapter 13 that operational selector switches for more than two inputs were primarily a matter of arranging the logic controlling the F.E.T. switches. The final system illustrates how simply this can be done using the hardware given here. A desire to actually construct and use a system capable of placing four independent traces on a single-beam oscilloscope is not prima facie evidence of megalomania; for example, one of the inputs can simply be connected to signal ground, thus providing a datum that is welcome in working with dc circuits using a vacuum-tube oscilloscope. Furthermore, the multiple traces can be convenient for demonstrating systems of the complexity of those in this chapter. As to their usefulness in actually working with such systems, caution is indicated: they can sometimes be helpful if used with discretion. The problem can become one of finding an investigator with a four-trace mind—but the final chapter is devoted to matters of this sort.

Figures 14.29 and 14.30. This system is an extension of the previous system exploiting the ability of a flip-flop to trigger a second flip-flop and the perfect number of possible states of two flip-flops for controlling four switches. It further exploits the complementary outputs of each flip-flop to make simple diode logic gates do the job in a very direct way. Logic driver circuits have been omitted for simplicity from the schematic. They appear in the block diagram and have a rightful place in practical systems; the price of omitting them here is that the operational switch will handle signals not exceeding about ±5 volts when the F.E.T. switches are driven directly from the 8-volt outputs of the flip-flops.

As the flip-flops permute through their possible states, there is in each state one and only one F.E.T. switch that is turned on because *both* of the flip-flop outputs connected to it are positive; it is this switch which is selected to conduct its signal to the amplifier. That is the way the selection logic works—those who choose to think in terms of "and gates" or "or gates for negative logic" clearly do so at their peril, for in this writer's experience seldom does the logic flow in anything like the same direction as the current, and thus perhaps began the great conceptual divide that has split the electrical engineering trade for two decades. Note that if it is important to operate the switches in a chosen sequence, the sequence can be more or less laboriously traced out and the operational switch inputs labeled accordingly. The intent here is not to disparage the field of logical design, but merely to illustrate that there are cases where it can be avoided, and should be.

Chapter XV

Recommended Laboratory Practice

This book is about hardware of a peculiar, brainy sort—it is proper that it close with a discussion of the practical and human problems of working with this hardware in the laboratory. There is much about practical work with electronic apparatus that is neither taught nor learned but rather acquired gradually, a process that most find to be a pleasant experience. There is the problem of how to proceed so as to get on with it while this sediment of expertise is accumulating.

The best approach is to purchase one of the five-amplifier operational manifolds now offered by the major manufacturers of operational amplifiers and related gear. Without the need to solder a connection or worry about power supplies, et cetera, these manifolds provide a patch panel that allows circuits to be connected temporarily as quickly and easily as they can be drawn. The utility of these universal breadboards grows with the experience of the user. Furthermore, careful construction and wiring practice make them superior in electrical performance to all but the most carefully designed instrument packages. The only obstacle is initial cost, which comes to about $500, including connection hardware and a selection of 1% computing components ready for use. Those who have read at all deeply in this book are in a position to decide whether their interest in operational technology justifies this outlay. If there is doubt, demonstrations or periods of trial use are easily arranged,

246

and are in fact directly relevant because a virtue of this technology is its experimental immediacy.

At the other extreme: microcircuit operational amplifiers and pairs of batteries to serve as bipolar power supplies are available for less than $10, but the tyro who elects to take this route should be prepared to invest quantities of his time, and be forewarned that there are more or less unpleasant realities, such as that an operating soldering iron has two ends differing markedly in the degree of comfort with which they can be grasped.

It should be noted that encapsulated power supplies suitable for up to ten operational amplifiers are available for about $25.

In any event, an oscilloscope is a necessity. At the very least the vertical amplifier should be direct coupled; identical vertical and horizontal channels are desirable, since X-Y plots are much used. The scope need not be fast or elaborate otherwise, although a good dc-triggered sweep is highly desirable. Sensitivity down to 1 millivolt/centimeter is convenient but not essential because a super dc preamplifier can be constructed from an operational amplifier as needed. In general, most of the oscilloscopes to be commandeered around the laboratory, or the schoolroom these days, are adequate—and *any* oscilloscope is better than none.

A 6.3-volt filament transformer can serve in lieu of a signal generator. At least one of the operational manifolds cited above provides 6.3 volts ac rms on its patch panel. A signal source of 60 hertz, approximately 18 volts peak-to-peak and roughly resembling a sinusoid is thus available; it is monotonous, but the price is unbeatable.

As to other gear, a volt-ohmmeter is nearly a necessity, even though most of the time it will be used as a simple continuity checker. Fortunately these instruments are easy to find if not always easy to borrow. It should be high on the list of items to be purchased because it is germane to electrical work of every sort; a corollary is that one should keep it locked up because, as the graduate students put it, its vapor pressure at room temperature is impressive.

There is a classic question of both practical and theoretical interest: what component value should I use? The correct answer is remarkable for its capacity to infuriate: that depends. Observe that resistors ranging from 1 ohm to 100 megohms are routinely available, and that this convenient variability is one of the strengths of operational technology. The question really reduces to: what should I try first to get something that works? There is an answer: 10,000-ohm resistors and 1-microfarad capacitors. This answer applies to making invertors and integrators with transistor operational amplifiers. There has been an effort throughout the book to answer this question ostensively in the examples used; this is really the only way it can be answered, since a fully formulated answer would amount to nothing less than a complete algorithm for the design of operational circuitry.

Obviously the choice of component value is informed by a range of considerations from the abstract to the brutally practical. Beginning with the latter, one should use what he has or can contrive to get most readily. This sounds crude but is highly advisable; it is often better to improvise with a component in hand that is off in value by a factor of 100 than to wait several days for the correct one. One of the blessings of operational technique is that impedance levels can be shifted to allow such substitutions.

On a still practical but slightly less brutal level: operational amplifiers have a specified maximum output current, frequently 2.2 milliamperes. If one seeks to make an invertor capable of driving its own feedback resistor and the input resistors of three similar circuits (that is, in a very fortunate phrase from the digital field, having a fan-out of 3), it behooves him to use $20K$ resistors throughout if signal swings of up to 10 volts are anticipated. There is seldom an advantage in using larger resistors than indicated by this kind of computation, unless something in the design dictates it, such as the need to achieve a given RC time constant with a given capacitor size.

As a rule, resistors in the range of 5 to $100K$ are suitable for transistor amplifier circuits. Above $100K$, F.E.T. amplifiers are called for to keep errors due to input current under control. A close reading of Chapter 9 on amplifier errors will do much to inform the choice of component values in its final, most refined stages. Even here, though, good practice favors the choice of standard values and even the use of configurations amenable to such standard values, as illustrated by the meter circuits of Chapter 8. Especially in these days when the cost of a precision resistor can exceed that of the amplifier with which it is used, intelligent selection of components merits attention. However, little more can be said except that a thorough understanding of the circuits themselves is the only firm basis for design.

Experimental work with circuits can be costly in time and emotional energy unless carefully steered in productive directions. Strictly speaking, it is impossible to so direct one's efforts; one can, however, avoid known unproductive practices. One should not spend unlimited periods at the bench; it is better to limit himself to half or three-quarters of an hour. The few seconds spent in refamiliarizing oneself with the experimental lash-up, far from being waste motion, are often the nucleus on which new questions crystallize. And given the proper questions, finding the answers is relatively easy.

The temptation to "fiddle" must be controlled. This does not mean that one must not fiddle, but that he be aware that he is thus rambling and how long he has been at it. The time should shortly come to step back from the bench and formulate a new set of questions. Experimental work should be a *conversation with the hardware*, full of polite but pointed interrogatives, and when it falters it should be broken off until new thoughts occur; the hardware is not affronted by these interstices.

A central paradox of circuit work is that it is inordinately difficult to remember the very last change that one has made to a circuit. An exorbitant amount of time can be spent in seeking out what suddenly "went wrong" with a circuit, when all along the cause has been some direct but unforeseen consequence of the latest "improvement" that was deliberately made. This sounds silly and in a sense it is, but the reality of it is so undeniable, that this forewarning is probably futile. By much the same unconscious mechanism that blinds one to his own typographic errors, it is extremely difficult to seek the cause of a malfunction in one's own no doubt inspired actions—it seems much more plausible at the time that a random failure has occurred. Such random failures do not happen often with modern electronic gear. There are some palliatives for this insidious form of pilot error, but they are no more than that:

1. Well-constructed breadboards reduce both the likelihood of accidental shorts or open circuits and the temptation to spend time searching for them.

2. Only one change is to be made at a time; make it explicitly and check that the result is as intended and *only* as intended—unnoticed consequences of a change are time bombs.

3. The circuit is to be returned to its original state after every change. If a change is to be permanent, mark up or redraw the working schematic to incorporate it.

4. Systematic record keeping can help but is time consuming and actually obstructive of the best work—the court reporter cannot be the judge and certainly not the prosecuting attorney.

Added to this list is a final suggestion that may sound crackpot but should be taken seriously: circuits are very elaborate mechanisms capable of a great variety of behavior and misbehavior. A human being working with even the simplest of the circuits in this book for the first time is working near the limits of his ability. *Do not be afraid to talk aloud to yourself.* It provides a kind of aural echo that yields additional information storage that is needed. The information theorist who first proposed that thought is the process of communicating with oneself has been taken seriously. Talking aloud provides another channel of self-communication that is imperative even for circuit experts when facing really complex problems. There is genuine truth in the complaint that one cannot hear himself think. At any rate the urge to talk aloud should not be suppressed as foolish; doing so gives evidence about the problem, not about the problem solver.

A regular feature of experimental work is that circuits behave in unexpected ways, most often apparently minor and not directly connected with the business at hand. The finest judgement is required to decide how far to pursue these anomalies; today's aberration has become the basis of tomorrow's system often enough that policy must be made accordingly.

Index

Figure references appear in *italic* type.

KIRBY, W.B.